ORIGINAL FIRST EDITION

ISBN: 978-3-98929-331-1

IMPRINT:
BOOK SHELTER GMBH
AUFHÄUSERSTRASSE 64
30457 HANOVER
GERMANY

INTRODUCTION

December. The streets are brightly lit, children and adults eagerly open their Advent calendars, and the sweet smell of cookies is in the air everywhere. But behind the 24 true crime stories of this book lies no sweet secret—only the darkest sides of reality: true crimes that will chill your blood.

This true crime Advent calendar takes you into a world where nothing is staged; everything really happened. Each story tells of lives irrevocably changed by violence, deception, or murder. These cases reveal just how thin the curtain between normalcy and horror really is.

The selection is diverse: gruesome serial murders, mysterious disappearances, and deadly crimes of passion. Some are internationally known, others almost forgotten—but each one is haunting in its own way, opening another "door" into the abyss of the human psyche.

What makes this Advent calendar unique is that each of the 24 stories are also available as videos. At the end of each chapter, you will find a QR code linking directly to a film adaptation of the case—perfect for when you're on the go or want to experience the story even more intensely.

This is not light reading. It is intended for those who are not afraid of the darkness, who seek to understand what turns people into monsters, and those who know that evil often hides where you least expect it.

So, open a new chapter each day, and confront a reality more terrifying and cruel than any nightmare.

Please note: The language of the videos should normally adjust automatically to the language settings of your device. If not, you can manually choose your preferred language in the YouTube playback settings. Otherwise, playback will default to English.

The illustrations in the book are for artistic purposes only. The people depicted are fictional, and any resemblance to real individuals is purely coincidental.

CONTENT

CASE

1

1. DECEMBER

December 1. While Christmas lights were being turned on in many American cities, children were enjoying their first chocolates from their Advent calendars, and radio stations were playing "Jingle Bells" on repeat, a door opened at an unassuming courthouse in Volusia County to reveal something entirely different: a nightmare that had played out behind a suburban front door. For Angela Stoldt, December first was not a festive day—it marked the start of her trial, a trial that was not about a simple crime but about a story that had stunned even seasoned investigators. A story filled with pain, isolation, and a murder so brutal in its execution that it was hard to believe a mother of two children had committed it.

Angela Stoldt was born on April 7, 1972, in Bangkok. Uniforms, rules, and her family constantly moving from one place to another marked her childhood. Her father was in the military, and her mother organized family life with a firm hand. Discipline was expected, and emotions were suppressed. Stoldt grew up in an environment where order meant everything, but love, closeness, and genuine security were rarely apparent.

Early on, she stood out for her reticence. She spoke little and hardly played with other children, whereas her younger sister Esther was livelier and more open; these differences caused a rift to develop between the two at an early age. Stoldt often felt neglected and then responsible when her parents went on business trips, as she had to look after Esther, even though she was still a child herself. This responsibility weighed heavily on her, deepening her loneliness and distrust of others.

When she was a teenager, her father was dismissed from service, and her family decided to move to Deltona, Florida, in the United States for a new chapter in their lives. There, at the age of fifteen, Angela Stoldt met a young man who was three years older, charming, loud, and exciting. For her, it was the first attention she received that didn't feel controlling. She fell in love. The relationship developed far too quickly, and soon she moved in with him, and they got married.

What should have been a new beginning turned out to be a repeat of old patterns. The man was not loving; he was controlling and violent. Stoldt told her family that he treated her like a prisoner. He beat her, humiliated her, and repeatedly threatened to kill her. Some time passed, and she lived between fear and hope. At twenty, she finally left him, ending her first marriage, and she was already scarred inside and out.

Shortly afterwards, she married again and had her first child with her second husband, but her happiness was short-lived. Stoldt developed mental health problems, namely an anxiety disorder and depression. These diagnoses weighed heavily on her because they did not come alone. Stoldt was born without a thyroid gland, which meant lifelong treatment with hormones and medication. The pills made her tired, sluggish, and often unable to even get out of bed. Her marriage broke down, leaving her with a small child and without an education, a job, or prospects.

In her desperation, she decided she would find a man who could support her financially. The motivation was not love, but the will to survive. At twenty-five, she married for the third time, and another daughter was born from this marriage. The family moved to Volusia County, into a house with a garden, on a quiet street with palm trees, the picture-perfect suburban idyll.

At first, everything worked out. Stoldt tried hard to be a good mother. She kept the house clean, took care of the children's school needs, and even tried to strike up conversations with the neighbors. But the medication she had to take had side effects. She suffered from panic attacks with increasing frequency, and she became suspicious, erratic, and sometimes lost her bearings, but she fought; she didn't want to give up.

Stoldt had an unusual hobby: she collected weapons. Her house was full of them—decorative rifles, old pistols, modern handguns; most of them were unloaded, but she had enough ammunition to change that at any time. Some found this disturbing; others in Florida found it completely normal.

In 2006, James Schiefer moved in across the street with his family.

He was a strong man with a friendly smile who worked as a limousine driver. His partner, Candy Medina, had been living with him for 17 years, and together, they had two children and a third from Candy's previous relationship. The children soon played with Stoldt's children, and the families became friends. They helped each other with shopping, barbecued together in the garden, and organized outings. James was funny, reliable, someone who appeared to be a rock in the surf.

Stoldt appreciated him, perhaps more than she wanted to admit.

But while she seemed to be experiencing a new beginning, things continued to simmer inside her. Her marriage was on shaky ground, and when her third husband finally left her, Stoldt was alone again, this time with two children, no education, growing debts, and frayed nerves.

She asked family and friends for money, but it wasn't enough. The mountain of debt grew, and then James came up with a proposal that would change everything.

James' proposal was unusual and risky. He had problems with the social welfare authorities, he explained, and suggested that Angela Stoldt be registered as his beneficiary for his disability pension. The monthly amount: $1,230. He promised her that he would give her $100 every month. For him, this meant more security in the bureaucratic jungle; for her, a small ray of hope in an increasingly bleak everyday life.

Stoldt hesitated. It sounded like fraud, like something that could have consequences, but James assured her that this was common practice, that no one ever asked about it. He was persistent and kept bringing it up until she finally gave in.

They drove to the social services office together, signed the necessary forms, and then went to the bank to open a joint account. James had a check dated in advance for the new account; everything seemed organized, almost professional. Stoldt felt uncomfortable, but she told herself, "It's only for a few months. Just until I get back on my feet."

But it soon became clear that James had no intention of sticking to the agreement. He regularly overdrew the account. Stoldt tried to stop him, talked to him, and asked him to be more careful, but James already had access to the card details and secretly withdrew money, often more than was allowed. Month after month, she watched as the account emptied and the debts piled up, yet she remained silent. Perhaps out of fear, perhaps out of dependence.

At first, James continued to pay the promised $100, but then his problems began. The social welfare office became suspicious and started withholding part of its payments. James' financial situation worsened dramatically; he was several months behind on rent and was facing eviction.

He became more nervous, restless, and aggressive in his tone. Discussions became increasingly frequent, and he demanded that Stoldt help him. He said she should ask her father for $4,000, but Angela Stoldt refused. Her father was old and sick, and she didn't want to drag him into this chaotic situation.

The relationship between the two neighbors, once friendly and trusting, began to deteriorate. What had previously seemed like help now felt like blackmail. James put Stoldt under increasing pressure, became loud, and accused her of abandoning him. For Stoldt, it was déjà vu—another man who dominated her, who made demands, who knew no boundaries.

In April 2013, Stoldt decided to end the advance payment option for the joint checks. She wanted out of this situation before it escalated, but she had no idea that it was already too late.

Early in the morning on April 3, she picked James up from work as agreed. Her children were in the back seat, and she drove them all home. The children went to bed, while Stoldt and James stayed in the kitchen having a drink and talking quietly. It was about money, as always, and about what she could still get from her father, and what James needed.

Stoldt had prepared something. Something she could hardly explain to herself. She had taken a medication, a sedative, from her father's house. She knew that it had a strong effect when combined with alcohol—it made you sleepy, paralyzed. Maybe she just wanted James to stop talking. Maybe she wanted to sedate him for a few hours, or perhaps, something more.

She secretly mixed the drug into his drink, and James soon realized that he wasn't feeling well. He felt dizzy and lost his concentration, so Stoldt suggested they get some fresh air. She put him in the car and drove off to the cemetery. There, between the graves, she stopped. The scene was eerie: thick fog lay over the grounds, and the trees cast long shadows under the light of the streetlamps. James sat dazed in the passenger seat, and Stoldt stared through the windshield.

Then she told him that she had canceled the advance option.

James exploded. Despite his dazed state, he started yelling, pounded his fist on the dashboard, and grabbed her by the arm. He demanded that she reactivate the advance option. He threatened her. Loudly. Directly. Just as she already knew. Just as she never wanted to experience again.

Stoldt reached behind her into a box of camping equipment. She had thought there was a screwdriver in there, but what she held in her hand was an ice pick. Without thinking, she stabbed him—right in the eye.

James screamed, jerked, and lashed out, but he didn't stop fighting back. She reached behind her again, this time for a cable. She threw it around his neck and pulled it tight. He gasped, struggled, and eventually fell silent.

Silence. Only her breathing. Her pulse, like a sledgehammer.

Then she stabbed him again in the other eye. Stoldt sat in the car, her hands shaking. Next to her: a lifeless body, his face covered in blood. The ice pick lay between the seats, the cable still wrapped around his neck. She had done what she never thought possible, and didn't know what to do next. For a moment, she thought about going to the police to confess everything, say that it was self-defense, that she just wanted to survive, but her thoughts were racing. Would anyone believe her? Her, the mentally ill, repeatedly divorced woman with two children, who took medication, collected weapons, and had just killed a man? Or would they think she was a danger to her children, to society?

She decided against it. No police. Instead, she grabbed a roll of plastic wrap she had bought at a discount store a few days earlier for "garden waste," as she had told the cashier at the time. She carefully wrapped James's head. Layer by layer, so as not to dirty her car. She drove home, her hands gripping the steering wheel tightly; her eyes fixed on the road. Her children were asleep upstairs, oblivious; it was late, almost three in the morning.

She parked the car in the garage. The air smelled of gasoline, metal, and old sweat. Stoldt pulled James's body onto a plastic sheet, inch by inch, with great effort. She wasn't strong and her back ached, but she had no choice. She went into the house and fetched a kitchen knife and then a saw, tools she normally used for crafts or for repairing old furniture. Now a dead body lay on the tarpaulin.

She started with the legs, cutting through flesh, tendons, and bones. It took hours, and the floor was bloody, and her clothes were soaked. She worked as if in a daze, mechanically, without a plan. When he was fully dismembered, she carried the pieces into the kitchen and opened the oven.

She didn't know exactly why she did it. Maybe she believed that heat could erase all traces, that fire could eliminate what is otherwise indelible. But when the oven started to smoke and a foul, acrid smell spread through the house, she realized: this was not the solution, it was a mistake.

So on to plan B. She put pots on the stove, poured water into them, and added the body parts. The result was a macabre soup. At the same time, she stuffed other parts into garbage bags and wrapped them in newspapers.

The next day, she drove her children to the forest, ostensibly to dispose of a dead deer she had "accidentally run over." The children, unaware, helped carry it. It was a sunny day, the birds were chirping, and among the trees, human remains disappeared into the undergrowth.

Back home, Stoldt cleaned the oven, burned clothes, and hid the murder weapon in the shed, but the smell remained. It settled in the walls, in the carpets, and in her hair. Her daughter asked her what it was. Stoldt replied, "A dead rat in the oven."

But she knew that excuse wouldn't hold up for long.

Meanwhile, Candy, James's partner, was waiting at home for news. James hadn't shown up for his next job. He had supposedly driven a customer to Tampa that night, but after that, there had been radio silence. Candy tried to call him with no answer. Finally, she reported him missing. The police took the report seriously. A grown man suddenly disappeared, with no message or sign of life; it was suspicious.

The officers issued a public missing person report. James' photo was published, along with a description: 6'0" tall, 265 lbs., brown eyes, brown hair, several distinctive tattoos, including the word "Gringo" on his neck and a skull with the Metallica logo on his calf. His family was convinced he would never just disappear, not without his children, and not without a word.

The police began investigating his professional environment. They found his car, parked and undamaged, on the premises of the limousine company. There were no signs of a struggle or evidence of a crime; his boss, Pitt Harington, seemed at a loss. Even a mechanic, Williams, who had last seen James, could not provide any new information, except that James had been addicted to gambling and had debts.

The investigation came to nothing, and in the meantime, Stoldt began to cover her tracks.

She drove to nearby parks and buried James' cell phone and driver's license under trees. She threw pots, knives, and plastic items into public trash containers. A doormat, soaked with something she didn't want to name, ended up in a lake.

But with each passing day, the pressure grew. She slept poorly and had nightmares, and stopped taking her medication for fear of appearing even more dazed. This only exacerbated her symptoms: paranoia, delusions, feelings of guilt. Repeatedly, she thought she saw James in her house, that he was back, that he was talking; her mind began to break down.

Then, on April 20, came the moment when the facade finally cracked.

On April 20, Esther, Stoldt's younger sister, called 911. Her voice was nervous and trembling, but determined. She said that Stoldt had been acting "strange" for days, and she seemed confused; she was talking about investigations and a heavy guilt. She had also hinted at wanting to take her own life, and that she had, in Esther's words, "done something terrible."

The police responded immediately. Officers were sent to Stoldt's house, accompanied by the mobile psychiatric service. Stoldt opened the door barefoot, her face gaunt, with dark circles under her eyes. She let the officers in but hardly spoke. When she did, she answered questions evasively or not at all. When asked to sit down, she just nodded and stared silently ahead; her gaze was empty.

A paramedic assessed her condition as "mentally unstable with suicidal tendencies." She was taken to a psychiatric clinic for observation. Even in the ambulance, Stoldt began to talk, confusingly, fragmentarily, but with recurring terms: guilt, corpse, fire, forest.

While Stoldt was under observation, the police obtained a search warrant. The next morning, a team of investigators conducted a thorough search of the house. What they discovered left even the most experienced among them speechless.

The walls were painted with strange symbols: pentagrams, crosses, and confused words written on the walls in red felt-tip pen. In one of the bedrooms lay crumpled prayer cloths, religious figures, and candle remnants. On a table lay an open notebook with illegible entries. In the living room, there were stacks of unopened mail, empty medicine packages, and used syringes. In the kitchen, the place where it had all begun between Stoldt and her victim, there was still a strange smell; a mixture of cleaning products, ashes, and something else. Something rotten.

In the oven, investigators found remnants of tissue. On the stove: a burnt pot with black residue. Next to the sink: a saw whose teeth were stuck together with a dark substance. On the garage floor, they discovered pale, dried bloodstains that had been doused with cleaning products. However, the cleaning had only been superficially successful.

The officers photographed everything.

They secured evidence. None of it was proof of a crime, not yet, but it was enough to question Stoldt again.

At the psychiatric clinic, she was initially uncooperative: silent, apathetic, seemingly absent; but after several days, something broke inside her. She asked for some paper and a pen, then she began to write.

She wrote about James. About the conversations. About the money. About the ice pick. About the cable. About the forest. About the fire. Everything was there, disordered and chaotic, but real. It was not a clear confession, but rather a feverish dream of memories, guilt, and fear.

The police took the statements seriously. They began to check the locations Stoldt had mentioned. In a remote wooded area near DeLand, they found several garbage bags buried under a layer of leaves and soil. Inside: human body parts. A thigh, a kneecap, and some ribs. In another bag: clothing–a shirt with the logo of the limousine company where he had worked, pants, and socks.

An initial forensic examination confirmed that these were human remains, and DNA samples were taken. That same week, confirmation came: they were parts of James Schiefer's body.

Stoldt was officially arrested, without the possibility of release on bail.

The news hit like a bombshell. The media reported with headlines such as: "Mother dismembers neighbor," "Florida woman cooked corpse on stove." Neighbors gave interviews, saying that Stoldt had "always been strange" but never aggressive. Others shook their heads, saying she had been "a good mother." No one had expected anything like this.

Meanwhile, the investigation continued. Stoldt led the officers to other locations. A park, a pond, a trash can behind a shopping center. There, they found James' driver's license, the shattered cell phone, and plastic bags with tissue remnants. She stated that she had deliberately kept replacing the cell phone's battery with a new one, so that it would appear to be active, and seem as if James was still alive and had recently thrown the items away himself.

The forensic expert confirmed that the bones matched the DNA. However, the cause of death could not be clearly determined as the material was too fragmented and destroyed. The skull was never found, and the upper body was missing.

With the confession, the locations where the remains were found, and the sister's statements, there was enough evidence to press charges. Angela Stoldt was charged with second-degree murder, tampering with evidence, and mistreatment of a corpse.

And it was precisely this case that was brought to court on December 1—almost exactly eight months after the crime. A case in which no one knew whether the truth would ever come to light.

The courtroom was simple, almost austere. There was no room for drama, yet there was an oppressive tension in the air. The spectator bench was filled with reporters, relatives, and curious onlookers. Everyone wanted to see who this woman was who had allegedly dismembered her neighbor and cooked him on her own stove. Angela Stoldt entered the courtroom dressed in black, with straight, dark hair and large, angular glasses. She appeared calm—too calm, some observers later said. Her gaze did not wander around the room; it was directed inward.

The lead prosecutor accused Stoldt of acting out of greed. James' monthly check for $1,230 was her motive, according to the indictment. Outwardly, she shared a joint account with him, but in fact, Stoldt had long since decided to get rid of James. The fact that she had purchased plastic wrap and rubber gloves hours before the crime was considered evidence of planning and intent.

The prosecution also presented witness testimony from her sister Esther, who reported Stoldt's strange behavior, and her 17-year-old daughter, who spoke of a strange smell in the house that was supposedly coming from a "dead rat in the oven." But later, her mother confessed to her in tears that she had killed James because he had threatened to kill her and the children.

Stoldt herself took the stand; her voice was calm but fragile. Repeatedly, she addressed the jury directly. She told of the threats, of the night in the cemetery, of the panic when James had grabbed her. She said she thought he was going to strangle her due to the way he had yelled at her and harassed her. She reached for an object in a box full of camping equipment, believing it to be a screwdriver, but it was an ice pick. It all happened in seconds.

"I didn't want to kill him," she said. "I just wanted to stop him."

She described how he continued to attack her despite her initial injury, how she found the cable and squeezed it in a moment of pure panic. She was afraid for her children, and that she would lose them if she went to the police, which was why she tried to deal with everything herself.

The prosecution did not accept this. They showed a video from the interrogation room, where Stoldt says that after James was dead, she took the ice pick again and stabbed him in the other eye. A cruel act that was difficult to explain as self-defense.

Stoldt said in court that she could no longer remember it. "Sometimes dreams and reality get mixed up," she whispered. "I don't remember what really happened anymore."

The interrogation was tough. The prosecution pointed out how often Angela Stoldt had lied to the investigators when she said she had last seen James on April 5. To Candy Medina, who had assured her that she knew nothing about the disappearance. To the children, she took them to the woods to "bury a deer."

"You didn't just kill him," said the prosecutor. "You then tried to make him disappear. Piece by piece. How could that have been an accident?"

Stoldt didn't cry. She didn't look at anyone, as if she were just waiting for it to finally be over.

The mood in the courtroom shifted. What had initially seemed like a tragic misunderstanding now began to appear as a cruel act. A planned murder, cleverly concealed, yet doubts remained. Her children seemed sincere, and her sister appeared genuinely shaken, causing many to wonder: was she the perpetrator, or the victim of a system that had left her alone?

At the end of the fifth week of the trial, it was clear: the charges would be upgraded. Second-degree murder became first-degree murder, premeditated, planned, and brutally executed; the turning point had been reached.

Angela Stoldt, a 42-year-old, thrice-divorced mother of two children, was now accused of being a dangerous murderer, but the verdict had not yet been handed down.

And what was still missing was James' head, and a clear answer to the question: Why?

The jury retired to deliberate: eight men and four women. For twenty-two days, they had heard witnesses, seen expert reports, watched videos, and read statements. Now the decision was theirs. Stoldt sat motionless in the dock. Her gaze was fixed on nothing. No trembling, no sobbing. Only silence.

The jury took just under three hours, and when they returned, everything happened quickly. The judge entered the courtroom, sat down, and asked the jury foreman to read the verdict. A tense, almost fragile silence reigned in the room. No one whispered. No one moved.

"We find the defendant guilty on all counts."

Second-degree murder. Tampering with evidence. Mutilation of a corpse.

Stoldt showed no reaction. No nodding of the head, no breakdown. Not even when the bailiff approached her and handcuffed her. She seemed as if her body was still present, but her mind was long gone.

The judge read out the sentence: life imprisonment without the possibility of parole. Plus 15 years for handling the corpse, and another 5 years for deliberately concealing the crime. A final verdict. No room for interpretation. No room for pity.

Angela Stoldt left the courtroom in silence.

Reactions were divided. Some spectators expressed sympathy, not for the crime, but for the woman who, due to her illness, may no longer have been able to distinguish between right and wrong. Others were outraged. "Anyone could have reported it," said a former neighbor. "But she chose to cook him."

Candy's family was relieved. They had waited months for answers, for justice. But the pain remained. James's head was never found, nor was his upper body. What exactly happened in the car that night will probably remain unclear forever.

Investigators later said that without Stoldt's statements, they would never have been able to track down the crime. Everything was too fragmented, literally and emotionally. "Without her confession," said one official, "we would never have known what happened to James."

Stoldt's children were never charged. The prosecution saw no evidence that they knew what they were carrying into the woods.

What remains is a case that stands out even among Florida's numerous true crime stories. Not only because of its brutality, but because of its absurdity, its tragedy, and its incomprehensibility. A woman, mentally unstable, a multiple failure, deeply overwhelmed, meets a man with debts, a gambling addiction, and his own demons.

Whether it was self-defense or murder may never be known with certainty.

After the verdict, Angela Stoldt was transferred to the Lowell Correctional Institution and housed in the security wing. It is a cold, sprawling facility in central Florida, surrounded by high walls, watchtowers, and double steel gates. There, in a cell without mirrors or personal belongings, she began serving her life sentence. There was no appeal. No interview. No public statements.

A few weeks after the trial ended, she underwent several psychiatric evaluations, according to her file. The reports spoke of emotional numbness, deep-seated anxiety disorder, and post-traumatic symptoms. One expert wrote, "Ms. Stoldt does not seem to deny what happened – but she cannot process it either." Another wrote: "Her relationship with reality is fragile. What she perceives as self-protection is interpreted by outsiders as cold-bloodedness."

In the public eye, memories of the case faded faster than one might expect. After the initial media shock, there were no further details, no revelations, no sensational interviews. Perhaps because no one knew what to make of this story.

Because it wasn't easy to tell. It was too complex. Too sad. Too real.

In internet forums, some speculated that Stoldt herself was a victim of abuse, neglect, and society. Others called her a monster, proof that madness and brutality often lurk behind the most inconspicuous facades. A few spoke of how quickly a web of poverty, mental instability, and social isolation can become deadly.

Watch the video

A profiler's opinion on this case

CASE 2

2. DECEMBER

December 2. While many families in the UK were opening the second door of their Advent calendars and looking forward to the upcoming holidays, a courtroom in Scotland handed down a verdict that felt colder than the frost on the streets. On this day in 2008, Peter Tobin was found guilty of the murder of 15-year-old Vicky Hamilton. A man who had hidden behind multiple identities, mingled with the homeless, and sought shelter in churches, but whose true identity was that of a serial killer. What began with a single body found in a chapel led to an abyss that even experienced investigators could hardly comprehend.

Britton Tobin was born on August 27, 1946, in Johnston, Scotland, the youngest of eight children. He was considered difficult from an early age. At the age of seven, his parents sent him to boarding school, but this did not improve the situation, and shortly afterwards, he was sent to a reformatory. What exactly led to this remains unclear, but those who later analyzed his life spoke of early signs of impaired impulse control, frequent lying, and a lack of remorse.

After his time in the institution, Tobin moved to Brighton, England, where, as a young man, he met 17-year-old Margaret Mountney. She was a typist, friendly, trusting, and impressed by his charm. They married in August 1969, but soon the attractive man turned into a controlling tyrant. Tobin beat her, isolated her, and controlled her every move. When he was arrested shortly afterwards for theft and forgery and sentenced to prison, Margaret filed for divorce. It was the first documented breakup; one of many that were to follow.

In 1973, he remarried. Sylvia Jefferies, a 30-year-old nurse, fell in love with his outward gentleness, and their son Ian was born that same year. A year later, their daughter Claire was born, but sadly, the baby died shortly after birth. This marriage was also marked by violence and intimidation. Sylvia left him in 1976, with her son in her arms and fear in her heart.

Then things quieted down around Tobin for a while. Not because he had changed, but because no one knew exactly where he was.

It was not until years later, when he was in his forties, that he reappeared—this time with Cathy Wilson. She was sixteen, vulnerable, and easily influenced. The two began a relationship, moved in together, had a child, Daniel, and married in 1989. But with their new life, the old pattern returned. Control. Isolation. Violence. Cathy was no longer allowed to go out alone; every step had to be "approved." It was life in a cage.

At the end of the 1990s, Cathy managed to escape with their son, leaving Tobin with contact to only one of his sons. Whether her departure was the trigger or just the last straw is unclear, but from that moment on, Peter Tobin finally dropped the mask. What he had kept hidden until then now came out uncontrollably.

In February 1991, fifteen-year-old Vicky Hamilton disappeared. She had traveled to Bathgate to visit her sister Sharon. It was the first time she had traveled alone by bus. A little adventure. Something special for Vicky—a journey into independence.

On February 10, a cold, snowy Sunday evening, she stood at the bus stop in Bathgate, opposite the police station, with a bag of chips in her hand. She had made sure she had enough money for the trip, and her sister had explained how to get to the bus, hugged her, and wished her well. Then, she was gone.

No one saw Peter Tobin drag her into his car. No one heard her screams. No one suspected that on that night, the paths of two people would cross in the cruelest way.

He raped her. He murdered her. Why exactly, one can only speculate. To silence her? Out of pure malice?

One thing is certain: he kept her handbag.

When Vicky didn't arrive at her mother's house, the family immediately began searching for her. The police were called in, and her face appeared on posters, in newspapers, and on television. It became one of the largest search operations in Scottish history, with thousands of tips and countless interviews, but no one knew that she was already dead, and that her killer had long since moved on.

The days following Vicky's disappearance were marked by hope and fear. Her family called hospitals, searched parks, talked to friends, and printed flyers. The police questioned passengers, bus drivers, and neighbors; it all seemed like a tragic misunderstanding: a teenager who had perhaps run away. But Sharon, Vicky's sister, insisted that wasn't like her. Vicky was reliable. Punctual. And she had been looking forward to returning to her mother.

Investigators began checking the area around the bus stop. The fact that she disappeared from a place directly opposite a police station was a cruel coincidence, or perhaps the very reason why no one suspected anything. Who would expect an attack there?

But Peter Tobin knew how to remain unobserved. He was experienced, manipulative, and dangerous.

He left Scotland shortly after the murder. He traveled to the southeast of England, to Margate, a quiet seaside town. There, he rented a house with a garden in a neighborhood where no one asked too many questions. He was "the man with the little boy" who sometimes played with him in the sandbox on weekends and occasionally pottered around the garden in sweatpants and flip-flops.

What no one knew was that beneath this sandbox, carefully poured, covered with concrete slabs and soil, lay Vicky's body, wrapped in bags, stowed away, and forgotten.

The neighbors thought he had built a play area for his three-year-old son. A harmless father. No one asked any questions. No one looked any closer.

At the same time, Tobin laid a false trail. On February 21, 1991, eleven days after Vicky's disappearance, her purse was found in Edinburgh, at the central bus station. The police then suspected that the girl wanted to travel to London and had perhaps run away. The investigation shifted from Scotland to England. From a possible crime to the case of a teenager who had presumably run away.

It was exactly what Tobin had intended. He had deliberately planted her belongings there to buy time and mislead investigators, and it worked. For weeks, the police searched in the wrong direction. Clues were followed, leads were checked, but nothing led to her.

Then came what no one said out loud, but many thought: maybe she didn't want to be found. Maybe she was just another teenage girl who had had enough of family problems: Her parents' divorce, the move, the new school. It fit the picture, at least on paper.

But Sharon knew better, and so did Vicky's mother. They didn't believe she had run away, but they had no proof, just a feeling. A feeling that eventually turned into grief.

A few months later, Vicky's mother died. The cause of her death was never fully clarified. Some said she couldn't bear the uncertainty. Others said her heart was too weak. But anyone who heard Sharon years later knew that she had died with the question of what had happened to her daughter.

In the years that followed, Vicky's face remained on missing persons posters. Newspapers regularly reminded readers of her, especially on anniversaries. The police took out the file several times and then put it away again. There were over 7,000 names in the investigation files, over 3,800 statements, and almost 500 investigation documents. Yet, there were no hot leads.

And Peter Tobin? His name never came up. He lived inconspicuously. Moved around. Worked here and there, sometimes with false papers, and always under the radar. To the authorities, he was a petty criminal, but not a sex offender, not a murderer. Not yet.

Because Vicky wasn't the only victim. It was early August 1991. Life was pulsating in the fields of Hampshire in southern England. Thousands of young people had flocked to the music festival, which brought new faces, new songs, and new stories every year. For many, it was a weekend of freedom, including Dinah McNicol, eighteen years old, from Essex.

She was a smart, vivacious young woman on the cusp of a new chapter in her life. She had just finished school, torn between wanderlust and career aspirations, she was considering whether to spend a year traveling or go straight to college. She hadn't received any answers from the universities yet, so everything was still up in the air, and the festival was the perfect escape from the waiting.

There she met David Tremlitt, and the two hit it off immediately. It was one of those fleeting, summery encounters that can feel intense, as if they were meant to last forever. On Sunday, August 4, they slept together in a tent. The next morning, they took it down together and decided to hitchhike part of the way back together.

They stood at the side of the road, tired but in good spirits. Then a car stopped. The driver was an older man, friendly and calm. It was Peter Tobin. He offered to give them a ride.

David got out earlier, and Dinah stayed; and that's when her nightmare began. What exactly happened in the following hours was never fully clarified, but one thing is certain: Dinah never made it home. Tobin had lured her into a trap. He tied her up and gagged her with her own handkerchief. He raped and killed her, just as he had done with Vicky, with cold-blooded calculation.

In Dinah's case, too, his plan was risky. She was firmly anchored in life, with family, friends, and a stable environment. She wouldn't just disappear without someone immediately asking questions. When she didn't return, her parents began searching for her.

And then something happened that confirmed their worst fears.

Withdrawals from Dinah's account were recorded at ATMs in Hampshire and Sussex in the days after her disappearance. Her family knew immediately that it couldn't have been Dinah. She was thrifty and would never have withdrawn so much money without reason.

The police began to investigate, but as with Vicky, there was no body and no clues. And Tobin? He had already moved on. The man who seemed to meet young women by chance was not out and about by chance. He was searching, and he knew how to disappear.

The search for Dinah went on for two months without success. Her relatives lived between fear, anger, and quiet hope, but with each passing day, it became clearer that she would not return.

For Peter Tobin, life went on. Unnoticed, unrecognized, free.

On August 4, 1993, exactly two years after Dinah McNichols' disappearance, Peter Tobin was tempted again. This time, he was living in an apartment in Leigh Park, Hampshire; inconspicuous and functional, a place no one would associate with a crime. But behind those walls, something was happening that would change the lives of two girls forever.

Two fourteen-year-old schoolgirls were out that afternoon to visit an acquaintance. The woman was not at home, and instead of turning back, they went to the next door: Peter Tobin's. Whether out of curiosity, good faith, or a harmless request, they knocked, and he opened the door. A polite man, who was calm and friendly, who had a little boy, his son, playing in the apartment; everything seemed normal.

According to later statements, it was also possible that the girls had responded to an advertisement seeking a babysitter. The atmosphere was relaxed until the door closed behind them.

No sooner were they inside than the mood changed. Tobin transformed. He pulled out a knife, tied up the girls, and forced them to drink alcohol. Then the nightmare began. He beat, threatened, and raped them. One of the girls was particularly badly injured. The pain, the fear, the helplessness—it was all overwhelming.

But then, a coincidence; his son woke up. The little boy ran through the hallway, and that soft, clumsy sound that would touch any parent's heart stopped Tobin. For a moment, he was no longer the perpetrator, but the father who feared his cover would be blown. What if the child had seen something? What if he spoke?

Tobin stopped. He quickly took his son out of the apartment, but before he disappeared, he turned on the gas tap in the kitchen. Perhaps he wanted to destroy himself and all the evidence. Perhaps it was a last, cowardly attempt to cover his tracks.

But his plan failed as the girls came to. They were injured and shocked, but alive. They managed to free themselves and go to the police. There, they told everything. Their statements were clear. The man they described was Peter Tobin.

But he had long since gone into hiding. He took his son to his mother's house and disappeared.

A few days later, he reappeared under a new name: Pat McLaughlin. McLaughlin was a seemingly broken, remorseful man who sought refuge with a religious community in Coventry. The Jesus Fellowship took him in, and in his new role as a devout outsider, he found the perfect cover.

This time, though, he wasn't quick enough; the media had his face. BBC Crimewatch broadcast his picture, and tips poured in. Finally, traces of a vehicle were traced back to him. After 40 days on the run, the search ended on May 18, 1994, in Brighton, where Peter Tobin was arrested.

He pleaded guilty to sexually assaulting the two girls and was sentenced to 14 years in prison.

For the public, the chapter was closed. A perpetrator had been caught, a criminal was behind bars, but no one, not even the police, suspected that Tobin's dark chapters were not yet written.

In 2004, Peter Tobin was released from prison early; it was a decision that would later be heavily criticized. A convicted violent criminal, registered sex offender, with a known propensity for deception and manipulation, was free again.

He returned to Scotland, where his name appeared in relevant registers, but he remained under the radar. The trail went cold; where he lived, what he did—no one knew.

Until the summer of 2006, when a small church in the heart of Glasgow became the scene of one of the most shocking discoveries in British criminal history.

Tobin showed up at the door of St. Patrick's Church, disheveled, unshaven, with a story like many others: he was homeless, sick, looking for something to eat and a place to sleep. The parishioners took pity on him. They offered him help, clothes, food a place to sleep. He pretended to be Pat McLaughlin, an old man with a broken gaze.

But behind the facade, he was hiding a plan. He knew that churches often provide a special refuge for the needy, but also for criminals. No one asked questions when someone spent the night in the sacristy. No one checked if and when someone came or went, and Tobin exploited this mercilessly.

In the church, he met Angelika Kluk. She was a 23-year-old student from Poland who had come to Glasgow during the summer holidays to earn money. She helped in the church, cleaning and doing odd jobs. She was friendly, helpful, and trusting; exactly what made her a target for Tobin.

He talked to her, asked her to help paint an old barn, and she agreed. On Sunday, September 24, 2006, they worked together for hours. Some parishioners saw the two of them together; it seemed harmless.

But then Angelika disappeared. She didn't come home for dinner, and her roommate was worried. People asked around and searched the area, but found nothing.

During the night, the Browns, who lived in the high-rise across from the church, heard a strange scream. Leeka Brown later described it as short but piercing, as if someone was being forcibly silenced. She got up, looked out the window, but couldn't see anything, and didn't think anything of it.

But Angelika was already trapped and helpless at that point. Tobin had ambushed her in the chapel, raped her, abused her, and finally killed her. Then he hid her body under the floorboards, right next to the confessional, a place that stands for forgiveness; the symbolism was cruel.

But he had made a mistake. Too many people had seen him with Angelika in the days before, and when the police began questioning people the next day, his name came up immediately. "Pat." The old man. The one who was always helpful.

But "Pat" was no longer there, Tobin had already disappeared. The police began digging—literally. On September 29, they found Angelika's body. Fingerprints found in the church led them to Peter Tobin.

The news shocked not only the community but the whole of Great Britain. A young woman was found dead, buried in a church, and the man who had lived among them was suddenly a wanted criminal.

David Swindle was a criminal expert with experience in highly complex and difficult investigations. He was convinced that the murder that had now been discovered was not an isolated case.

The brutality with which Angelika had been killed suggested years of practice, and Tobin's past was too opaque. Swindle wanted to know: What had this man done in the years before?

While the search for Tobin was in full swing, he went into hiding in London—in a hospital, where he pretended to be James Kelly, supposedly a paramedic. He complained of chest pains, numbness, and weakness; it was all just a pretext.

But Dr. Nick Lossow, who examined him, became suspicious. The symptoms did not match the test results. In addition, the man avoided eye contact. When a nurse recognized the face of the supposed patient on the news, it became clear: they were dealing with the most wanted man in the country.

On September 30, 2006, Tobin was arrested.

Officially, this was initially only for violating the reporting requirements for sex offenders, but the investigators used the time to their advantage. DNA traces at the crime scene matched Tobin's profile, and his fingerprints had also been found in the church; the evidence was overwhelming.

In March 2007, the trial for Angelika's murder began. Tobin pleaded not guilty and claimed that the sex with Angelika had been consensual. It was a last-ditch attempt to deny responsibility, but the court did not believe him.

After a six-week trial, he was found guilty of murder, rape, and misleading the authorities. The sentence: life imprisonment, with the earliest parole after 21 years. For many, this was not enough.

But senior police officer David Swindle had long since come up with a bigger plan. He launched Operation Anagram, which aimed to reconstruct Tobin's entire life. The goal was to compare missing persons with his whereabouts, because one thing was clear: a man who kills so cold-bloodedly has probably murdered before.

The officers discovered two places that were particularly interesting: Bathgate and Margate, places Tobin had lived in the 1990s.

In the summer of 2007, investigators began searching Tobin's old house in Margate. At first, they found nothing until they examined the sandbox in the garden. Neighbors recalled that Tobin had allegedly built it for his son, but under the concrete slab, investigators discovered plastic bags. Inside: human remains.

Forensic examination revealed that there were two female bodies.

And there was something else: a handbag was found nearby, which Tobin had apparently kept as a disturbing trophy. DNA analysis confirmed that it was Vicky Hamilton, who had been missing since 1991. Shortly afterwards, the second body was identified as Dinah McNicol.

Two families who had waited sixteen years for answers finally learned the truth.

On December 2, 2008, Tobin was sentenced to another life sentence for the murder of Vicky Hamilton. A year later, on December 16, 2009, the third conviction came: life imprisonment for the murder of Dinah McNicol.

Three victims. Three verdicts. Three life sentences. But was that all? Or did Tobin have even more lives on his conscience?

The police suspected that Tobin was responsible for far more murders than could be proven against him. Some estimates put the number of possible victims at up to 40. But only what could be proven forensically could be proven. Many clues had been covered up, and other bodies were never found or misidentified. And Tobin? He remained silent. Never showed remorse and revealed nothing.

Peter Tobin died of cancer on October 8, 2022, at the age of 76 in a prison hospital in Edinburgh.

Watch the video

A profiler's opinion on this case

CASE 3

3. DECEMBER

On December 3, the common room of the residential complex in Lorton was transformed into a small winter wonderland. Colorful garlands decorated the walls, Christmas carols played from the speakers, and the smell of baked goods mingled with the giggles of children scurrying around among the festively dressed adults. For many, it was the most wonderful evening of the year; an opportunity to get in the mood for the upcoming holidays, laugh together, and forget about everyday life for a few hours.

But what began as a carefree Christmas party was to turn into a nightmare that very night, because that evening, five-year-old Melissa Brannen disappeared without a trace.

Melissa lived with her mother, Temmy, in one of the apartment buildings that belonged to the festively decorated residential complex. Temmy had started a new life in Virginia after divorcing Melissa's father and worked as an accountant. She was well known in the neighborhood as friendly, helpful, and always ready to listen to others. And Melissa was a lively, bright child whom almost everyone in the residential complex knew.

That evening, she was full of anticipation for the party. There were cookies, games, and music; everything that makes a child happy. Temmy chatted with acquaintances while Melissa darted around the rooms with other children. Everything seemed perfectly normal.

Around 10 p.m., Temmy wanted to leave. She asked her daughter to get her jacket while she said goodbye to some neighbors. Melissa nodded, disappeared toward the coatroom, and never returned.

At first, Temmy thought Melissa might have been distracted by a game or gone into one of the side rooms with one of the other children. She called out to her, looked under the tables, in the hallways, even in the restrooms, but there was no sign of Melissa anywhere. The minutes passed, and Temmy's uneasiness turned into sheer panic. When other adults joined the search and no one could find the girl, Temmy grabbed the phone.

A few minutes later, the first police officers arrived. They joined the search, combing through the entire building together with the residents, searching the corridors, hallways, and the surrounding area. It soon became clear that Melissa hadn't just fallen asleep somewhere or hidden herself. She was gone.

More than 300 volunteers joined the search that same night. The police initially assumed a classic scenario: a small child gets lost in the dark, runs into the nearby forest, and can't find her way back. But this theory became less and less likely with every passing hour.

Melissa knew the area well; she had been there often. Besides, it was a freezing cold December night, and there was no indication that she would have wanted to stay outside for long. And the most disturbing detail: her jacket was missing. The girl had apparently left the common room, but no one had seen where she went or with whom.

The police began systematically questioning all the guests at the event. Nearly 200 people had been present that evening, but no one had noticed Melissa leaving the room. Nor had anyone seen her being accompanied by anyone. It was as if she had disappeared without a trace, from the middle of a crowded building, while other people were laughing, dancing, and celebrating.

Temmy insisted that she had no enemies in the neighborhood, no one who would want to harm her or her daughter. Nevertheless, investigators pursued one of the most common theories in such cases: a possible abduction by the father. It quickly became apparent, though, that he had been thousands of miles away in Texas at the time of the crime. The lead was a dead end.

Instead, the officers decided to massively expand the search area. The residential complex was located on the edge of a large forest, and now this area was also being searched. Hundreds combed through the forest, while others inspected every building in the vicinity, but even after hours of intensive searching, there was not a single usable lead.

By the next morning, the search had grown into one of the largest police and volunteer operations Lorton had ever seen. Yet, there was nothing: no trace, no clue, no sound. Only an open window in the boiler room caught the investigators' attention. It was unusual and a small detail that would later prove to be significant.

Investigators began interviewing all the residents of the apartment complex in person. Over 400 people lived there, and the police spoke to each and every one of them in the hope of finding at least a small clue. Residents were asked to remember anything that might be unusual, any strange movements, any strange behavior.

Several women independently mentioned a man named Caleb Hughes. He worked as a janitor in the apartment complex and had also attended the event that evening. These women reported that he had behaved conspicuously; he had approached them, made suggestive remarks, and gotten too close to them despite the presence of their partners. What was particularly striking, however, was how much attention he had paid to the children. Several parents had an uneasy feeling about him, although no one could say anything specific.

When investigators questioned Temmy again, she also confirmed that Hughes had spoken to her that evening. He had asked about Melissa and even offered to accompany the girl to the bathroom so that Temmy could chat with the neighbors undisturbed. In retrospect, these gestures no longer seemed friendly, but calculated.

The police wanted to question Hughes that same night, but he was nowhere to be found, either at the apartment complex or at home. His wife opened the door and said he hadn't returned yet. It was hours later when the officers returned to his home, and this time he was there.

Hughes explained that he had not come home until around 1:30 a.m. The problem was that he had left the Christmas party at 11 p.m. So where had he been in the meantime? He replied that he had made a detour to buy beer, which is only allowed until midnight in Virginia.

Then things got strange. When the officers asked to see his work clothes, Hughes said he had just washed them, including his shoes. The police insisted on taking the clothes with them for examination. They noticed that the shoes in particular had been thoroughly cleaned. In addition, part of the soles had been cut off. Officers also found an empty knife sheath and a leather belt. When asked about the missing knife, Hughes had no answer.

With each new detail, the investigators' suspicions grew. The clothes were taken to a special laboratory, where forensic technicians used luminol testing to reveal traces of blood on Hughes' shoes. The amount was small, presumably greatly reduced by washing, but it was enough to underscore the seriousness of the situation. Nevertheless, definitive proof of a crime was still lacking.

The police took Hughes to the station, where he was interrogated for hours. Despite the incriminating evidence, he insisted on his innocence. He claimed that he did not know Melissa and had never seen her. However, this statement contradicted those of several witnesses, including Temmy, who confirmed that Hughes had spoken to her daughter.

When the officers confronted him with this and said, "We know you're lying," Hughes remained cold as ice. His response: "Prove it."

Since there was no concrete evidence, he had to be released for the time being. The next morning, however, investigators sought another conversation with his wife; this time in his absence. She mentioned a striking detail: she had noted the mileage on his car on the evening of the party, and when he returned, the odometer showed about 19 kilometers more than before.

This information was a turning point, as it directly contradicted his statement that he had only wanted to buy alcohol. The nearest store was only a few minutes away. Thanks to the mileage information, investigators were now able to calculate the search radius, an area of about 40 square kilometers around the residential complex. Police, volunteers, and even the military began systematically searching the area. Helicopters, search parties, and divers—everything was deployed.

At the same time, the police arranged for all the apartments in the residential complex to be searched, with the residents' consent. The hope was that Melissa might have been hidden or locked up somewhere. But no trace of her was found either in the buildings or in the adjacent forest.

The only thing investigators could find near the scene was an inconspicuous shoe print under the window of the boiler room, the room where the window was open. The print clearly belonged to an adult, and no children's footprints were found nearby. The trail led directly to the parking lot.

The theory gained weight: Melissa had not gone out alone. Someone had carried her.

The search for clues in Caleb Hughes' car was intensified, this time with the support of the FBI. His wife, who officially owned the vehicle, agreed to the renewed search. Investigators used state-of-the-art forensic methods, including luminol testing, and discovered traces of blood under the driver's seat, on the pedals, and even on the windshield. Although no DNA could be extracted, that wasn't all they found.

An experienced forensic scientist decided to secure even the smallest particles by systematically scanning all surfaces of the car with adhesive tape. Among all the dust, dirt, and dog hair, he noticed a different kind of fiber—fine, black-colored rabbit hair. A sample from Temmy's winter jacket, which was made of exactly the same material, confirmed the suspicion: it was exactly the same fabric.

Even more revealing was a single blonde hair, which was also found on the passenger seat. A comparison with Melissa's hairbrush revealed a match. The crowning glory, however, was the discovery of hundreds of tiny fibers in red and blue, exactly the colors of the outfit Melissa had been wearing on the evening of her disappearance.

But that wasn't all: a forensic technician remembered a comment made by his wife, who suspected that such garments might have been available at the JCPenney chain. After looking through old catalogs, she found the outfit in question in a Christmas edition from the previous year. The FBI immediately contacted the company. Although the model was no longer available, it turned out that it had been sold exclusively through catalogs, in exactly 7,000 copies.

The investigators obtained a list of all purchasers. One of them, a man from Kentucky, had accidentally bought the set in the wrong size. The unworn garment was still in its original packaging at his home, a stroke of luck. The fibers were compared and matched 100% with those found in Hughes' car. What's more, the outfit had a unique, specially developed shade of blue with the color code 887, another distinctive feature.

An extensive comparison with almost 8,000 other fibers confirmed that only two samples were identical: the fibers in the car and the original garment from Kentucky. This made it clear that Melissa had been in that car.

But one problem remained: there was no body, and according to state law, someone could only be charged with murder if either the body or the crime scene was found. Therefore, the prosecution decided to charge Hughes with child abduction, knowing full well that this would result in a lighter sentence.

During the trial, Hughes continued to insist on his innocence, but the evidence was overwhelming: bloodstains, fibers, hair—everything pointed to his guilt. It took the jury only seven hours to find him guilty. The sentence: 50 years in prison, the maximum penalty for child abduction in this case.

Melissa was never found.

Although the verdict had been handed down, many questions remained unanswered. Caleb Hughes had been convicted, but the crucial piece of the puzzle, knowledge of Melissa Brannen's whereabouts, was still missing. Investigators hoped that the man in custody might still confess, but Hughes remained stubborn. He repeated over and over that he had nothing to do with the girl's disappearance. His stance remained unchanged even under pressure, during lie detector tests, and confrontations with incriminating evidence.

Four years after the verdict, something unexpected happened. An employee of an energy company working on a power line in the region discovered a red piece of fabric resembling clothing in a remote lake. Police divers were immediately sent to the site, but this clue also led nowhere; no further traces, no body, no new insights.

Time passed. Eight years after Melissa's disappearance, Temmy remarried. She built a family life with her new husband and raised four children with him. Although she took her husband's surname, she remained known by her old name in everyday life. In conversations, in letters, in public appearances, she wanted Melissa, if she was still alive somewhere, to be able to find her easily.

In 2019, almost 30 years after the crime, Caleb Hughes was released from prison early for good behavior. At that point, he had served just over half of his sentence. The news hit like a bolt from the blue. Many who still remembered the case were shocked that the man was now free again. Hughes himself never appeared in public after his release. He settled in an unknown location, subject to parole conditions that did not include the obligation to disclose his whereabouts.

For Temmy, this release was a heavy blow. She had hoped that she would at least get justice by Hughes having to serve his full sentence.

But she continued to fight, quietly but persistently. She campaigned for missing children, supported other families in similar situations, and spoke to organizations working to improve legislation on child abduction.

Melissa Brannen is still officially considered missing. There is no gravestone, no memorial, no final closure. Only a photo of a little girl with blonde hair that remains in many family albums, at the police station, and in the hearts of those who have never forgotten what really happened on that December 3.

Watch the video

A profiler's opinion on this case

CASE 4

4. DECEMBER

On December 4, 1998, the small town of Hopewell, Missouri, was shaken by a tragedy that remains a mystery to this day. It was a cold Friday morning, the sky was overcast, and there was a smell of burning wood in the air. At around 6:30 a.m., a local teenager reported that a fire had broken out in his family's mobile home. The police and fire department arrived quickly, but what they found on the scene was far more than a routine fire.

In the remains of the burned-out trailer, they discovered the body of Rita Politte, a single mother of three children. The fire department was able to quickly extinguish the flames, but for Rita, any help came too late. Her body was burned beyond recognition, but what could still be seen was disturbing: Rita had apparently not died in the fire. A forensic scientist noticed marks on the back of her head that indicated she had been struck with a blunt object, a clue that she may have already been dead when the fire broke out.

The news spread quickly in the small community. Rita was a well-known and respected woman, one who had lovingly cared for her children and never lost her zest for life despite difficult times. She was particularly close to her youngest son, Michael, who was just 14 years old at the time. It was Michael himself who ran out of the trailer that morning, screaming for help in a panic and trying to alert someone.

At first, it looked like a tragic accident. A fire caused by a faulty stove or a dropped cigarette, at least that's what people thought in the first few hours, but the closer the investigators looked, the clearer it became that something was wrong.

Michael stated that he had spent the night in the trailer with his mother and a friend. He woke up, smelled smoke, and immediately tried to find his mother, but the smoke was too thick. He ran outside to get help, but the friend who had also spent the night there was nowhere to be found.

In interviews, Michael appeared distraught but calm. Some officers noticed that he did not cry, while others thought he spoke in unusual detail about the events. His clothes smelled of smoke but showed no visible signs of burning, and although it was cold, he was not wearing a jacket when the police arrived.

At first, his statements were believed; after all, he was only 14, seemed honest, and the loss of his mother was obviously a shock. But on the same day, investigators began to suspect that something was wrong, and soon their suspicions turned to the boy who was mourning his mother.

Michael was immediately questioned intensively. At first, he was treated like a witness, a child who had experienced a tragedy, but soon the tone changed. The police took him to the station and interrogated him for hours, without a lawyer or an adult by his side. His parents were divorced, and Michael's father, Ed Politte, lived about 90 miles away. While Michael's sisters were already grown up and had moved out of the family home, his parents shared custody of Michael, and he lived alternately with his father and mother.

The investigators wanted to know when he had last seen his mother, what they had done the night before, and whether there had been any arguments. Michael repeatedly replied that they had simply watched television together, eaten pizza, and then gone to sleep. But the more questions they asked, the more nervous he became.

The police began to look for contradictions in his statements. Why had he claimed to have seen his mother sleeping when, according to the coroner, she must have already been dead at that point? Why wasn't he burned if he had supposedly been in the same room? And where was his friend, who was also supposed to have been in the trailer that night?

At the same time, investigators began analyzing the scene of the fire. According to expert reports, the fire had most likely started in the bedroom where Rita had been found. The officers found traces of accelerant, specifically gasoline. This made it clear that it was not an accident, but deliberate arson.

Now it was clear to many investigators that someone had set the fire to destroy the evidence. The fact that Rita had suffered severe head injuries before the fire suggested that she had been murdered, and the fire was probably intended to cover up the evidence. The only question was: who had a motive? And who had even been in the vicinity?

The police began to investigate her surroundings. They checked Rita's past, her relationships, her work, but everything they found was unremarkable. No conflicts, no enemies.

Her family consisted of her ex-husband, two adult daughters, and Michael, who had been staying with her that week.

For the police, the circle of suspects was therefore small, and although there was no direct evidence against him, everything focused more and more on the 14-year-old son. Public opinion quickly followed suit. Rumors spread in the small town. Why wasn't he crying? Why did he remain calm? Why wasn't he injured?

Investigators decided to test the boy for traces of gasoline, and indeed, tiny residues of it were found on his shoes. For the police, this was the turning point. Suddenly, it no longer mattered how weak the evidence was. It was something, and they were determined to hold Michael accountable for the crime.

On January 6, 1999, just a few weeks after his mother's death, Michael Politte was officially charged with first-degree murder. The prosecution assumed that the then 14-year-old had beaten his mother to death with a hard object and then set the fire to cover up the crime scene.

It was a difficult decision because the evidence was anything but clear. There was no murder weapon, no eyewitnesses, and no DNA evidence that clearly linked Michael to the murder; only the gasoline residue on his shoes, and even that could not be definitively linked to the fire. After all, Michael and his friends had used gasoline before to remove old paint from their bicycles or to make campfires. In a rural area, this was nothing unusual.

Nevertheless, the prosecution insisted on charging the teenager as an adult. In Missouri, this is possible; in particularly serious crimes, minors can also be tried in adult court. This meant no juvenile sentence, no special protection. Only the full penalty, as for an adult offender.

The decision was justified on the grounds that Michael was allegedly "mature enough" to understand the consequences of his actions. But critics, even then, noted that the decision was based less on maturity than on the desire to present a guilty party.

Michael was remanded in custody to a juvenile detention center while awaiting a trial that would determine his entire future life. During this time, he received little psychological care and no intensive support. The boy, who had just lost his mother, was labeled a murderer even before the trial had begun.

When the time finally came, the prosecution focused almost entirely on circumstantial evidence: the boy's behavior after the fire, his unclear statements, and the gasoline trace analysis. Everything was presented as suspicious. Even his calmness and the fact that Michael had shown no emotion were interpreted as evidence of coldness and guilt.

The defense, on the other hand, had a difficult time. Michael came from a modest family, and financial resources were limited. The lawyers who defended him had little experience with murder cases. In addition, there was no investigation by the defense, no independent expert opinions. They relied almost exclusively on the police's findings, even though these findings were questionable.

Despite all the uncertainties, the jury ultimately decided to convict. Michael was convicted of second-degree murder—not premeditated murder, but intentional killing. The sentence: at least 30 years in prison with no chance of early release. Michael was 16 years old at the time, and he was to spend the next three decades behind bars for a crime he claimed he never committed.

Criticism began to emerge shortly after the verdict. Local journalists, lawyers, and even some former investigators began to ask questions. How could a boy with no history of violence, no motive, and no clear evidence be sentenced to 30 years in prison?

Michael's family didn't give up either. His father, sisters, and some close friends believed in his innocence from the start. They began collecting documents, reviewing old statements, and making contacts with journalists. The first articles expressing doubts about the boy's guilt appeared in the local press just a few years after the verdict. But it would be years before the case received wider public attention again.

A key factor in this was an organization called the Midwest Innocence Project, a non-profit initiative that campaigns on behalf of people who have been wrongfully convicted. Members of the organization became aware of the case through a newspaper article and contacted Michael. He was open and cooperative, and immediately agreed to release all documents. It quickly became clear to the project's lawyers and volunteers that something was wrong.

The new investigations revealed numerous flaws in the original proceedings. For example, the alleged traces of gasoline on Michael's shoes had never been independently verified. When a forensic laboratory was commissioned to conduct new tests, the results were surprising: it was most likely not gasoline, but a similar substance found in wax and household products.

It also turned out that the police had failed to follow up on important clues or had done so inadequately. For example, a friend of Rita's had testified that she had been afraid of her ex-partner in the weeks before her death. She had even said that she felt she was being watched. However, this man was never questioned in detail, let alone investigated.

The role of the friend who had stayed overnight at Michael's house was also never really questioned. He later admitted that he had not told the police the whole truth because he was afraid. He felt pressured to portray Michael's behavior as suspicious, even though he himself had never seen anything that indicated a crime.

Another problem was the cause of the fire itself. Initially, it was assumed that the fire had been started deliberately, and a so-called accelerant was said to have been used. But modern fire experts came to a different conclusion: there was no clear evidence of arson. Rather, it could have been an accident, caused by a fallen candle or a technical defect, for example.

All these new findings led the Midwest Innocence Project to file an official motion to reopen the case. The grounds: new evidence, flawed investigations, inadequate defense, and a fair trial that Michael had never received.

But the justice system was slow to respond. The motion was rejected several times on the grounds that the new information was not "sufficiently decisive." Michael remained behind bars, but public pressure grew. Podcasts, television shows, and online articles reported on the case with increasing frequency. Michael's fate moved many people, not only because he had been so young, but because the entire trial seemed like a mistake from the outset that no one wanted to correct.

In 2021, almost two decades after the conviction, what Michael and his supporters had been waiting for so long finally happened: the appeals court agreed to review the case. Finally, everything that had been ignored or dismissed over the years would be considered.

The new hearings dragged on for months. The public followed them with great interest, because in the meantime, the case had become symbolic of the failure of the justice system. Numerous experts appeared, including forensic experts, criminologists, and psychologists. They all came to similar conclusions: the evidence against Michael was vague and unreliable, or the investigation methods were now outdated.

The interrogation methods used at the time were also viewed particularly critically. Michael was 14 years old, alone, and without a lawyer or his father. The interview lasted for hours, and he was confronted with a sudden accusation to which he reacted emotionally. From the perspective of modern interrogation techniques, the approach was highly questionable.

The sum of all these doubts, contradictions, and new findings was overwhelming. Finally, the court declared that the original conviction was based on an incomplete and unfair trial, and officially overturned the verdict on December 14, 2021.

After 18 years in prison, Michael Politte was a free man.

When Michael left prison, his sisters, his lawyers, and representatives of the Innocence Project were there to greet him. Images of his release were broadcast in the media. Many celebrated this day as justice belatedly served, but Michael himself seemed composed. “I’m happy to be out,” he said. “But there are many others like me who are still waiting.”

During his imprisonment, he had studied the justice system intensively, reading books and studying legal documents. Today, he is actively campaigning for reforms. Above all, he wants to ensure that minors are never again interrogated without a lawyer, one of the most important lessons learned from his case.

Despite his newfound freedom, many questions remain unanswered for Michael. His mother’s death was never reinvestigated. To this day, he does not know for sure how she died, and no one has been held accountable for this loss.

With the overturning of the verdict, Michael’s nightmare was theoretically over, but the reality was different. Even though he was now free, his innocence had not been officially established. The court had overturned his conviction because the trial had been flawed, not because he had been proven innocent. That meant no compensation and no official admission of guilt on the part of the state. This was difficult for Michael to bear. After 18 years behind bars, he was released into a system that offered him no help whatsoever. No money, no therapy, and no prospects. People who come out of prison often have difficulty finding their way in the outside world, and for someone who was imprisoned as a child, this step is even more difficult. Michael had to learn how to use a smartphone, how to apply for a job, and how to live as a free man.

The stigma had not disappeared either. Although the media celebrated his release, not everyone believed in his innocence. Some still saw him as the boy who had killed his mother. Discussions arose on social media, with some posts expressing doubts that his acquittal was justified, but Michael decided not to let doubt or fear guide him. He began to speak publicly about his story, attending events and giving talks at schools and universities. He warned of the dangers of a justice system that treats children like adults, that makes quick judgments without considering how easily a suspect's life can be destroyed.

Michael's commitment earned him recognition. Various initiatives, including the Midwest Innocence Project, joined him in fighting for legal changes. Their goal: to allow interrogations of minors to take place only in the presence of lawyers or guardians in the future. They also demand that juveniles in pretrial detention no longer be treated like adults.

But Michael also worked personally to build a life for himself. He completed vocational training, found an apartment, and tried to rebuild ties with his family, especially his sisters, with whom he had shared the most difficult time of his life. While he waited behind bars for justice, his sisters maintained contact with the outside world. They sent him photos, mementos, small reminders of the world he had lost. In every message, there was a silent promise: "We believe in you. We are waiting for you."

Michael Politte's case was later covered in several documentaries. Today, it is seen as an example of how quickly a teenager can become a scapegoat when evidence is lacking and authorities feel the urge to close a case quickly.

Many who have followed his journey see him not only as a victim but as a fighter, someone who has not been broken despite all the adversity.

But the central question remains: Who killed Rita Politte, or was it just an unfortunate accident? In the authorities' files, it remains an unsolved case.

Watch the video

A profiler's opinion on this case

CASE

5

5. DECEMBER

December 5. Winter had arrived in many American cities. Children were throwing their first snowballs, stores were decorating their windows with fairy lights, and there was a sense of anticipation in the air as Christmas approached. But in a quiet suburb of Merced, California, the Stayner family was not in a festive mood. For them, this day was not part of the magic of Advent—it was the day their world began to crumble. Because on this day, they realized that they might never see their son again.

On the morning of December 4, 1972, seven-year-old Steven Stayner left the house as usual to go to school. He carried a backpack that seemed almost too big for his petite frame and said goodbye to his mother with a quick wave. No one knew that this would be their last goodbye—at least for many years. When Steven did not return home that afternoon, a nightmare began for the family that seemed to have no end.

The police were notified, neighbors questioned each other, and soon flyers with the missing boy's picture were posted all over Merced, but every lead came to nothing. It seemed as if Steven had been swallowed up by the earth. While his parents, Delbert and Kay, clung to every straw, his older brother Cary, then eleven years old, began to quietly withdraw from reality. To the public, Steven was now one of many missing children. To his family, he was everything.

No one suspected that the little boy was being held captive just a few miles away in a remote cabin by a man with a specific plan, disguised as a kind-hearted soul. While Christmas lights sparkled outside, Steven began years of torment in the care of a man who pretended to be his new guardian.

And while Steven longed to return home, something else was growing inside his brother Cary, a feeling of invisibility, of being overlooked, which would soon develop an ominous momentum of its own.

Steven was still a child when he began to remember a new name. One that had not been given to him by his parents, but had been forced upon him by his kidnapper. "Dennis Parnell", that was the name given to him by his kidnapper, Kenneth Parnell. On December 4, Parnell's accomplice, Edward Murphy, approached Steven with a mixture of feigned sympathy and perfidious calculation, handed him a religious brochure, and lured him into the getaway car that was waiting nearby.

Parnell was a seemingly harmless older man with thinning hair and a calm voice who pretended to be an employee of a religious organization and claimed that Steven's parents no longer wanted him. It was a lie, so carefully packaged that it sounded credible to a seven-year-old child.

Parnell knew what would follow: a new life with a false identity, in a remote house, far away from Merced. There, he began to systematically manipulate Steven. He gave him gifts, promised him freedom, passed him off as his "son", and at the same time set in motion a perfidious system of control, fear, and abuse.

While the media published initial reports about the missing boy, Parnell tried to cover his tracks. He dyed Steven's hair, did not enroll him in school, and moved with him to other places. In the eyes of the outside world, the new boy at his side was simply a late-born son, and no one asked any questions. And Steven? He was confused, overwhelmed, but also dependent, because Parnell was the only one he had left. And so, Steven began to live the lie.

Meanwhile, normality did not return to the Stayner family. The children's room remained untouched, and the bicycle still stood against the wall. Cary, the big brother, began to change. He hardly spoke about Steven anymore. Instead, he withdrew into himself, drawing in his notebook for hours and observing animals in the garden, and then focusing exclusively on that. His parents understood their son's quiet behavior, but no one suspected that a shadow was already growing in Cary that would take deeper root than anyone could have imagined.

The years passed, and seven-year-old Steven became a teenager who hardly knew who he really was. In public, he called himself Dennis, but deep down, he remained Steven, a child who was missing, who was being searched for, but who could hardly find himself anymore. Parnell moved with him across half of California, sometimes living in trailers, sometimes in cheap motels or remote houses. Never for long, never anywhere where anyone asked too many questions.

Parnell left Steven alone if he didn't complain, and resorted to control and violence when the boy rebelled. He sent him to different schools, forbade him from having contact with his peers, and didn't let him write letters. Yet Steven tried as best he could to create a semblance of normality. He took care of pets, helped neighbors carry groceries, and learned to do minor repairs. Outsiders thought he was a shy but polite child. No one suspected the circumstances in which he lived, and that his "father" was not his father at all.

At the same time, Cary was also changing. The years without Steven were like an endless noise to him. Outwardly, he became calmer, quieter, but inside, a storm was raging. He developed compulsive rituals, began to suffer from depression, and withdrew completely. At school, he was considered a loner with dark thoughts. His classmates kept their distance, and his teachers tried to intervene unsuccessfully. His brother's disappearance had left a deep wound in him that grew larger with each passing year.

The family tried to stick together. Christmas was celebrated every year, but it was never the same as it had been before Steven's disappearance. Every gift under the tree was overshadowed by his absence. The empty place at the table was a reminder of what had been lost. Hope faded, but it did not die. His parents never gave up.

And Steven? He slowly began to realize that what he was experiencing was not normal, that what was being done to him was wrong, but he did not know how to escape. Because his life was a prison without bars.

The older Steven got, the more restless Parnell became. The boy he had once been able to control was becoming independent, asking questions, and contradicting him. Steven was now almost 14 years old, too big, too loud, too visible. It became clear to Parnell that if he wanted to maintain control, he needed a new child. A boy who was still malleable, innocent, and easier to make dependent on him.

And so, he began to pressure Steven. He asked him to kidnap children himself—a perfidious step that was meant to show how far his manipulation went, but Steven refused. Again and again. So often that Parnell finally hired someone else: a teenager named Randall Sean Poorman, a friend of Parnell's. In February 1980, they kidnapped five-year-old Timothy White on his way home from school.

Steven couldn't take it anymore. He saw himself in Timothy. A little boy, full of fear, full of questions, and crying for his mother. That night, while Parnell slept, Steven made a decision: he would run away. Not for himself. For Timothy. Maybe for both of them.

On March 1, 1980, they seized an opportunity. Steven took Timothy by the hand, left the remote house in Ukiah, and searched for help for hours. Finally, they reached a police station in the city. When the officer asked him who he was, he replied hesitantly, "I think... my name is Steven. Steven Stayner."

In Merced, the ensuing phone call signaled the return of a ghost. For seven years, Delbert and Kay had lived between hope and despair; now their son was back. The media pounced on the story. A hero, a survivor, a boy who had not been broken. But behind the heroic narrative lay another pain: Who was Steven now? And what had become of the boy who had left home on December 4, 1972?

Cary watched his brother's return in silence. The media pointed their cameras at Steven, interviewed him, and turned him into a symbolic figure, while Cary stood in the shadows. This solidified something within him: a feeling of not being seen. Not heard. Not important. It was the quiet beginning of a dangerous development.

Steven was home. Physically, at least. But the child who had left seven years earlier no longer existed. In his place was a teenager with scars that no one could see, but which resonated in every sentence, glance, and silence. The family tried to return to normality, but what does normality look like when seven years are missing?

Steven had difficulty adjusting. School was a challenge, not only because of the material he had never learned, but also because of the looks he got. Classmates either admired him or avoided him, and teachers treated him like a fragile object. At home, everything was familiar, yet strange. His childhood bedroom was smaller than he remembered. The furniture was still there, but he no longer fit in.

He started smoking, drinking, and got into trouble with the law. Nothing serious, but enough to worry his parents. Steven struggled with his identity. Was he a victim? A hero? A normal teenager? None of it felt right. In interviews, he often downplayed his experiences. He didn't want to be seen as the boy who was stolen, but as someone who was back.

Cary observed all of this. Silently. While the world talked about Steven, Cary became increasingly withdrawn. In his room, he collected newspaper clippings, scribbled dark sketches in his notebooks, and read about serial killers. He developed a fascination with violence that he didn't show to anyone. Perhaps because it promised him power in a world where he felt powerless.

The family recognized the imbalance but didn't know how to address it. The attention Steven received was understandable, but it made Cary invisible, and that feeling gnawed at him. Year after year, like a slow poison that penetrated deep into his mind.

Steven seemed to build a life of his own over time. He married at twenty, became the father of two children, and worked as a laborer. He rarely spoke about his years with Parnell, almost never about what he had to endure there. But the scars remained—in his behavior, in his nightmares, in his need to please others, and at the same time, never really feel like he belonged.

In 1991, Steven Stayner died in a motorcycle accident at the age of 24. The public reacted with shock. Newspapers reprinted his photo, reminding people of the kidnapping and his return. Many saw him as a tragic figure, but for his family, it was more than that: a second, this time final, loss.

Cary Stayner was 30 years old at the time. Quiet, polite, and unassuming. Outwardly, he never seemed to have fully stepped out of his brother's shadow, but inside, something else had long since matured. A dark obsession, fueled by years of rejection, loneliness, and pent-up anger.

In 1999, Cary struck. In a national park in California, he brutally murdered a young woman and two female tourists. Just weeks later, he confessed to the murders and revealed that he had been fantasizing about killing for years. The media once again pounced on the Stayner family. Two brothers, two extremes: one a victim who became a symbol of survival. The other a perpetrator who became the epitome of the inconceivable.

The story of the Stayner brothers became a tragic allegory for what trauma can do, not only to those who suffer it, but also to those who seem to be in the background. Because in reality, Steven's abduction had changed the lives of the entire family forever.

When the Christmas lights lit up again in Merced on December 5, hardly anyone remembered the day it all began, the first day without Steven. But for the Stayner family, that day was forever associated with a profound turning point, a point at which normal life came to an abrupt end and was replaced by years of pain.

Steven had left and returned, only to be lost forever later on. Cary had stayed, but drifted further and further away inside. Two brothers who became victims in completely different ways—one through violence, the other through silence and invisibility.

What if Steven had never been kidnapped? Would Cary have led a different life? Would he ever have committed murder? Or was the darkness within him independent of what happened to his brother? Questions to which there are no answers, but which leave a bitter aftertaste.

Watch the video

A profiler's opinion on this case

CASE

6

6. DECEMBER

December 6 is considered a day of giving in many regions of the world. It was St. Nicholas Day; the day children put their boots outside the door, families baked cookies, and fairy lights decorated the windowsills. In Austin, Texas, the city was in the midst of the pre-Christmas season. The nights had grown cooler, but the sky above the city remained clear. Soft Christmas music played in the shopping malls as customers strolled through aisles filled with special offers.

On this evening in 1991, a small yogurt shop on West Anderson Lane also had a quiet, almost sleepy atmosphere. “I Can’t Fight This Feeling” by REO Speedwagon played softly in the background as four girls between the ages of 13 and 17 waited for the shop to close. Two of them, Jennifer Harbison and Eliza Thomas, worked at the shop regularly; for them, it was a typical weekend evening. Sarah Harbison, Jennifer’s younger sister, and her friend Amy Ayers were visiting and waiting to drive home together.

The atmosphere was friendly. The girls laughed, told stories, and refilled the yogurt machines for the last time. There were hardly any customers at this time of night; the few who did come in grabbed a cup to go or stayed only briefly. The shift was due to end in a few minutes, a normal evening in an unremarkable shop.

But no one could have guessed that this evening would not end peacefully. That this St. Nicholas Day would not end with sweets, but with a nightmare. A nightmare that was brewing behind the friendly facade of a yogurt shop, and that would change four families forever. Around midnight, a patrol officer noticed smoke coming from West Anderson Lane. The smoke was billowing from the entrance area of the yogurt shop. Within minutes, firefighters arrived. The windows were fogged up, and the lights inside had already gone out. The men broke down the door and made their way through acrid smoke and flickering embers.

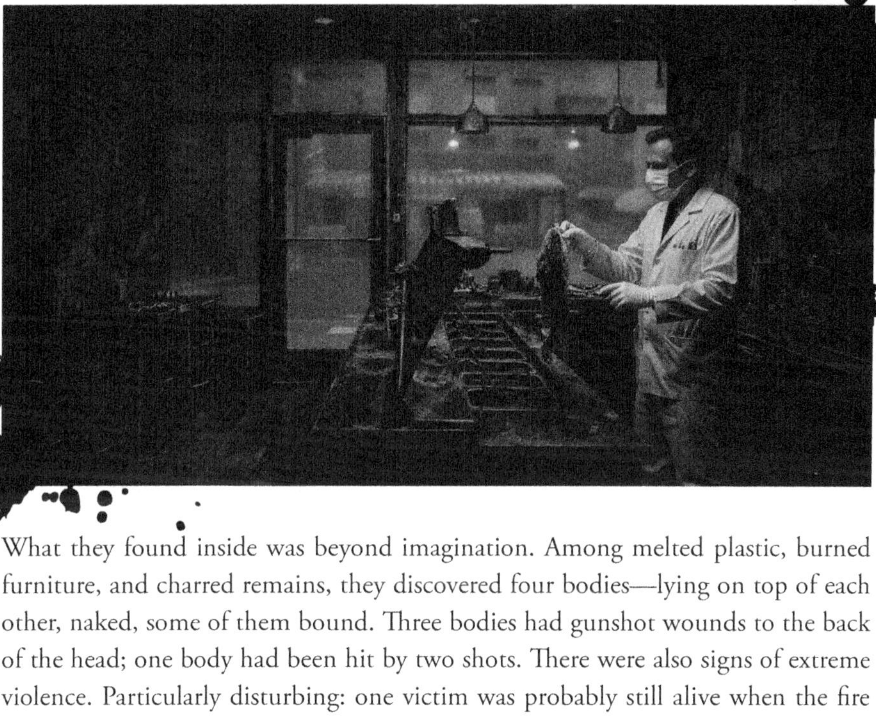

What they found inside was beyond imagination. Among melted plastic, burned furniture, and charred remains, they discovered four bodies—lying on top of each other, naked, some of them bound. Three bodies had gunshot wounds to the back of the head; one body had been hit by two shots. There were also signs of extreme violence. Particularly disturbing: one victim was probably still alive when the fire was set.

That same night, the crime scene was cordoned off over a large area. Forensic investigators, crime scene technicians, and fire experts arrived.

In the early hours of the morning, onlookers began to gather. Rumors spread quickly; was it a robbery, a crime of passion, a ritual murder? The police remained tight-lipped. Little was known. No surveillance cameras, no eyewitnesses. Just four young girls who had been brutally murdered, and a town that suddenly found itself in the midst of a nightmare.

The four victims were identified the next morning. Jennifer Harbison, 17, was a popular student and captain of the track team. Her younger sister Sarah, who had just turned 15, was considered bright and had a dry sense of humor. Eliza Thomas, also 17, had big plans; she wanted to study veterinary medicine. And Amy Ayers, only 13 years old, was the youngest victim. She had been in the store that evening on a whim, just because she wanted to accompany her friend.

The families were torn from their quiet lives overnight. There was no warning, no explanation, just a phone call that changed everything. The girls' parents arrived in the course of the morning and had to be guided through police cordons. Some broke down, others stood silently, staring at the charred facade of the store. No one could comprehend how a place where yogurt was sold and laughter rang out had become the scene of one of Texas's most heinous crimes.

The police set up a special commission. Investigators combed the area, interviewed neighbors, collected ashes, hair remnants, and DNA, but the fire had destroyed most of the evidence. There were indications of an accelerant, probably gasoline. The victims had been tied up, and some evidence pointed to sexual violence. It was a crime with chaotic and at the same time methodical elements; a contradiction that left investigators at a loss.

The media reported nationwide. Pressure on the police increased, and the city demanded answers; the parents demanded justice. Deep down, everyone was asking themselves: Who could be capable of such a thing?

What the investigators did not make public, however, was that there were some clues as to possible suspects. An anonymous witness had mentioned two young men who had been in the vicinity shortly before the store closed. Others spoke of strange figures who had been seen in the store on several occasions, but none of the clues were concrete enough to arrest anyone.

Days turned into weeks. The funerals of the four girls were attended by large crowds. Entire school classes came, as did teachers, neighbors, and people from other cities.

The coffins were closed. The details that emerged from the initial investigations were so difficult to bear that even the police officers received psychological counseling.

One particularly disturbing finding concerned Amy Ayers, the youngest of the four. The first shot had not killed her. She was probably still alive when the second shot was fired. The exact sequence of events could not be reconstructed, but the picture was clear: she had suffered. The idea was unbearable—for the family, for the public, for the investigators.

The press soon dubbed the crime "The Yogurt Shop Murders." A name so banal and tangible that it stood in stark contrast to the horrific content. But even with a name, the crime remained faceless for a long time; without a perpetrator and without justice.

It was not until two years later, in 1999, that the case began to move forward. The police had never given up; officers had spent hundreds of hours working through old clues, using new technologies, and comparing DNA profiles. A new lead pointed to four young men, all of whom had been between 15 and 17 years old at the time. They had previously been noticed in the vicinity of the store, had committed minor offenses, and one of them, Maurice Pierce, was carrying a gun at the time of the crime that was the same caliber as the one found on the victims.

Investigators arrested Pierce, Forrest Welborn, Robert Springsteen, and Michael Scott. The interrogations of Scott and Springsteen in particular led to a dramatic turn of events: both confessed. Scott said he had held two of the girls while Springsteen raped them. Afterwards, they set the fire to destroy evidence.

However, the manner in which these confessions were obtained soon became the subject of fierce criticism. Scott's interrogation had lasted over 20 hours, without a lawyer or his parents present. He was still a young man at the time, mentally unstable and intimidated. He later testified that he had been under pressure. Springsteen's statements also appeared contradictory in parts. There was no DNA evidence, no eyewitnesses, no clear motive, only these incriminating statements.

Despite the doubts, the trial went ahead. Springsteen and Scott were convicted and sentenced to life imprisonment, based almost exclusively on their own statements. The public was divided; some were relieved that someone had finally been brought to justice, while others doubted whether the right men were behind bars.

The victims' families also had mixed feelings. They wanted justice, but not dubious convictions. And the longer the case dragged on, the more their fear grew: what if the real perpetrator was still at large?

In 2008, almost two decades after the crime, there was a shocking twist. New DNA analyses, carried out using state-of-the-art methods, showed conclusively that the DNA found on Amy Ayers' body did not belong to Robert Springsteen or Michael Scott. It was the DNA of an unknown man. The case collapsed, the convictions were overturned, and the men were released.

The news spread like wildfire. After years of believing the case was closed, everything was now up in the air again. The police had to justify themselves once more, for the way the interrogations were conducted, for the lack of material evidence, and for an investigation that was based primarily on confessions that now appeared questionable.

For the victims' families, it was another blow. First the loss, then the apparent justice, and now the realization that the perpetrator might still be at large. That the real killer had never been brought to justice. That which they had thought was the end was only another interim result.

Austin changed over the years; it grew and became more modern, but in the minds of many, December 6, 1991, remained a sharp cut, a day that changed everything. The Yogurt Shop Murders became a dark chapter in the city's history, a case that was not forgotten even decades later.

To this day, no one has been definitively convicted. And while files gather dust and witnesses remain silent, an oppressive void remains: four young lives extinguished and a perpetrator who was never named.

The victims' families have never forgotten their daughters. Pictures still hang in schools today, and scholarships bear their names. But the memorial plaques tell only part of the story. The other part—the part that may never be fully told—is about what could have been prevented. About trust that was broken. And about a promise that has not been fulfilled to this day: the truth.

Watch the video

A profiler's opinion on this case

CASE 7

7. DECEMBER

December 7. For many Americans, this date is inextricably linked to the tragic events of Pearl Harbor. But on December 7, 1988, a tragedy took place in Los Angeles. Amidst the pre-Christmas hustle and bustle of the city, another day of filming was being prepared on the set of Lethal Weapon 2.

Bob Samuels was supposed to spend the day there as a camera assistant, but he was not there. On December 7, Bob Samuels was brutally murdered in his home. His body was not discovered until December 9.

What initially appeared to be a robbery soon turned out to be something much darker: a cold-blooded crime. The woman who spoke to investigators in tears was the same woman who would later make national headlines as the "Green Widow": Mary Ellen Samuels.

The story begins in a typical California suburban idyll. Bob grew up in modest circumstances, surrounded by orange groves. He developed a passion for photography at an early age and soon found work in the film industry; he was hardworking, reliable, and well-liked. Only his personal life didn't seem to be going well, until he met Mary Ellen Gurney again: the prettiest girl in school, his unattainable childhood sweetheart.

Years later, the two met again. She was divorced, a single mother with her daughter, Nicole. He was charming, successful, and ready for a family. The relationship began like a fairy tale. They married in 1980, and Bob adopted Nicole. Mary Ellen Samuels, as she was known after the wedding, moved into his house in the San Fernando Valley, but life there was not what she had expected. There were no red carpets, no spotlights, just everyday life.

Bob tried everything to make his wife happy. He even opened a sandwich shop for her so she would have something to do, but Samuels was bored. She didn't want to make sandwiches; she wanted to be desired. Soon she began attending parties, meeting new men, and dressing provocatively. Her daughter, Nicole, quickly became part of this new world: clubs, alcohol, and revealing clothes; mother and daughter became a team that was more interested in attention than morality.

Samuels used men as she saw fit. Her marriage to Bob slowly, but surely, fell apart. In 1986, she moved out and took Nicole with her, living off Bob's money, and already planning her next move. Bob was now thinking about divorce, but for Samuels, that would have been a financial disaster. Being a widow, on the other hand, would pay off.

But you don't commit murder alone. Samuels looked for a tool, and found it in a young man in love who didn't realize how much he was being manipulated. And so, a deadly plan bloomed.

On the evening of December 7, 1988, Bob Samuels returned home tired from work. He undressed and stepped into the shower, unaware that this would be his last evening. When he came out of the bathroom, he was surprised by a hard blow to the head from the butt of a rifle. Bob fell to the floor, unconscious, but still alive.

The murderer placed a pillow over Bob's face, pressed it tightly against his head, took aim, and pulled the trigger. The shot was muffled, stifled by the fabric. Bob Samuels died in the hallway of his own home, just two months after his fortieth birthday.

To cover up the crime, the apartment was hastily ransacked; drawers were torn out and objects thrown on the floor. It looked like a burglary, but to the trained eye it was immediately clear: the chaos was staged, and nothing of value was missing.

After Bob Samuels' murder, Samuels' life seemed to be unfolding as she had imagined. She was a grieving widow with a bulging bank account, living in her murdered husband's house, and having no qualms about flaunting her new wealth. The investigators had a bad feeling, but no evidence. Samuels seemed to have committed the perfect crime—a murder that looked like a botched burglary, staged by an inexperienced perpetrator who had vanished into thin air.

But the story wasn't over yet. Jimmy Bernstein, who had sacrificed himself for Nicole and believed he had to protect her, began to have doubts after the murder. He became increasingly restless. The young man felt that he had been used, and he was right. Nicole had turned away from him, and Samuels no longer showed any interest. Bernstein had blood on his hands, no girlfriend, and no prospects. He began to make hints to friends, acquaintances, and neighbors, and Samuels heard about it.

The danger that Jimmy would go to the police was real. Samuels understood immediately: she had to eliminate the threat and the danger before everything was in danger of being exposed. Her second plan was just as cold-blooded as the first. With this murder, she wanted to divert attention away from herself as much as possible.

She made sure she was in Cancun while the murder was being carried out.

Through an acquaintance, she came across Paul Gau, with whom she discussed the murder plans. She told him that Bernstein was blackmailing her. She also reported that Bernstein was selling drugs to minors, which made Gaul very angry because his little brother had been killed by drug dealers, and he was very angry about it.

So, he accepted the job in exchange for payment and teamed up with Priestly Ray Edwards to carry out the crime. Samuels provided her car for the job.

On the morning of June 27, 1989, Gaul and Edwards drank themselves up in a bar, made an appointment with Bernstein, and lured him into the car under the pretext that they wanted to rob some drug dealers in Frazier Park. In a remote location, they killed Bernstein by strangulation. When he asked, "Why?", Gaul replied, "Because you talked too much."

They threw Bernstein's belt, inscribed with the name "James," out of the car.

They threw his body into a remote pond, and his identification papers were later carelessly discarded on the street.

After a prearranged phone call with a coded message, Samuels returned from Mexico.

It took the police almost a month to find the body. When they searched Bernstein's apartment, they found evidence linking him to the murder of Bob Samuels, gaining momentum for the investigation.

The discovery of Jimmy Bernstein's body brought movement to a case that had previously been at a dead end. Investigators determined that Bernstein and Samuels had been more than just casual acquaintances. The first clues to a possible murder plot came to light, but the crucial piece of the puzzle that connected everything was still missing.

The turning point came thanks to a mistake. One of the two men who had killed Bernstein, Paul Gall, was not careful enough. He bragged to those around him about his "crime", talking about money and revenge. An acquaintance contacted the police anonymously, who then placed Gall under surveillance and eventually arrested him. During questioning, Gall broke down after a short time. He told them about Samuels, her greed, and her promises. Above all, he told them about the car she had provided.

When the investigators visited Samuels again, she was no longer a grieving widow. There was a new sports car in her garage, and the house was furnished with expensive furniture. She herself had changed her appearance—bleached her hair, had beauty treatments done, and wore flashy jewelry. Rumors circulated in the neighborhood about parties, loud music, and constant visits from young men. Samuels enjoyed the limelight, and she knew she was provoking people.

When the police questioned her about her relationship with Bernstein, Samuels acted surprised and denied any connection, but she had lost control. The investigators had Gall, they had Darrel Edwards, they had clues, and then they stumbled upon the life insurance policy. A contract for $500,000, taken out a few months before Bob Samuels' death, with Mary Ellen Samuels as the beneficiary.

The case took a new turn in the media. The story of the "Green Widow", as she was soon called, made headlines. When she was arrested on January 26, 1990, her apartment was searched, and investigators discovered a Polaroid photo taken in Cancun by her boyfriend at the time. It showed Samuels naked on a bed, her body covered only by $20,000 in cash, with a broad grin on her face. The Los Angeles Times reported on it with the words: "She was clothed only in her husband's blood money." She thus became a symbol of a woman who was willing to stop at nothing to get what she wanted.

She was accused of inciting the murder of her husband and of being an accomplice to the murder of Jimmy Bernstein. Her daughter Nicole was also questioned, but she remained silent. Now of legal age, she refused to make any statement.

The charges were clear, but the defense tried everything to portray Samuels as a victim of domestic violence. It was a game of emotions, memories, and tears, but the evidence was overwhelming: money flows, witness statements, life insurance, and her own greed.

The trial of Mary Ellen Samuels began in the spring of 1990 amid intense media attention. People lined up outside the courthouse in Van Nuys to catch a glimpse of the woman who was now considered the epitome of the cold, calculating widow in California. Her appearance in court was carefully staged: expensive suits, understated makeup, and an expression somewhere between innocence and superiority.

The prosecution focused on establishing a clear motive: money, attention, and power. They called witnesses who had attended Samuels' parties, including young men whom she had ensnared with gifts, alcohol, and promises. Particularly damning was the testimony of a former friend of Jimmy Bernstein, who recounted how Samuels had deliberately manipulated young, unstable men in order to use them.

Central to the trial was the photo showing Samuels a few days after her husband's death: smiling and surrounded by money. The prosecution used it skillfully as the picture said more than a thousand words. The jury appeared shaken when the photo was shown. The discrepancy between the alleged pain of a widow and this openly displayed decadence was too obvious.

Samuels' defense tried to paint a different picture. They presented her as a woman who had been trapped in an abusive marriage, who had suffered psychologically for years.

Contrary to her lawyer's recommendation, Nicole testified on behalf of her mother, also claiming that Samuels had been violent, which his relatives credibly refuted, and there was no evidence of violence in the relationship. Friends and colleagues of Bob Samuels also described him as a quiet, loving man who had sincerely loved his family.

Another key issue was the extent to which Samuels had gone to stage her innocence. The police reconstructed how she herself had left messages on Bob's answering machine to give the impression that she knew nothing about the murder. It was an almost movie-worthy script that she had written, but it was no longer convincing.

On the fifth day of the trial, Paul Gall took the stand. In handcuffs and under heavy guard, he described how Samuels had contacted him through an intermediary. He spoke of cash in envelopes, of promised protection, and of a planned third murder if necessary. It was a shocking picture, and it showed Samuels for what she really was: not just a perpetrator, but the driving force behind a web of lies, manipulation, and violence.

The prosecution concluded its argument with a sentence that burned itself into the memory: "She wanted a new life, but without witnesses." The jury retired, and just three hours later, the verdict was in: guilty on all counts.

Samuels was sentenced to death. California had not sentenced a woman to death in years, and now she was one of the few. But, while the world outside looked at her with outrage or fascination, she showed no remorse. Her face remained expressionless. No tears, no wavering.

After Samuel's conviction, there was no calm. The case had shaken the entire country, but the investigation was not over.

Paul Gall, the hit man Samuels had later hired, was now himself in custody. During his interrogations, he revealed details that painted an even darker picture.

Gall stated that Samuels had not only recruited him, but had instructed him with alarming matter-of-factness to also eliminate Jimmy Bernstein. The police later found handwritten notes in Gall's apartment with schedules, addresses, and even a rough escape route.

It was almost naive how carelessly Gall had left his traces behind. But it was also an expression of how much he had relied on Samuels' promises: that she would protect and take care of him. However, when he came under suspicion, all contact broke off. Samuels refused to make any statements about him. Gall was left alone and finally broke down under the pressure of the police.

The public reacted with horror to this turn of events. The fact that Samuels had not only had her husband killed, but also the young man who had carried out the murder on her conscience, made her, in the eyes of many, a symbol of a cold-hearted, manipulative character. Newspapers reprinted the aforementioned photo, this time with the caption: "She laughed while others died."

Legally, however, the second crime had little impact. Samuels had already been sentenced to death. For the prosecution, however, it was an important piece of the puzzle in showing the extent of her behavior. The double standard with which she played the grieving victim on the one hand and had people killed in cold blood on the other.

In the years that followed, Samuels remained in a California prison. Her appeals failed, and her lawyers tried to have her sentence commuted without success. Her cell was small and sparse, but decorated with pictures from fashion magazines. Even in prison, she tried to stage herself. She gave few interviews, remained vague, and avoided any direct responsibility.

Mary Ellen Samuels spent her days in California's women's prison in a cramped space that had little to do with the life she had once dreamed of. The glittering world of Hollywood was far away, the glamour forgotten. What remained was the image of a woman who had two lives on her conscience and showed no remorse.

The particularly well-known photograph was published in all the media: Samuels, smiling, lying on the bed, surrounded by bundles of cash. The press gave her a name that stuck: "The Green Widow". Green like the money that meant more to her than any life.

Watch the video

A profiler's opinion on this case

CASE 8

8. DECEMBER

The morning of Tuesday, December 8, 2009, was cool and clear in Statesboro, Georgia. It was exam time in the small university town, and while many students were holed up in libraries or cafes with their books, Danielle Davis was already up early. The 19-year-old freshman at Ogeechee Technical College had a stressful week ahead of her, but she was excited. In a few days, she was supposed to drive home to be with her mother, who was undergoing risky heart surgery. Her love for her family was unwavering, and no one who knew her doubted that Danielle would keep her promise.

By noon, Danielle's mother was already in the hospital, ready for surgery, but Danielle didn't show up. Her mother tried in vain to reach her, but calls went unanswered, and when Danielle's grandmother, Dale, also got no answer, her concern grew into sheer panic. Danielle was reliable; she would never have been late—especially on such an important day.

Dale finally turned to the dorm administration. Her request was simple: someone needed to check if her granddaughter was okay. No one was prepared for what followed. When the manager opened Danielle's door at around 3 p.m., he was met with a sight that left him speechless and reeling into the hallway.

Police investigator Jody Steford was on patrol that afternoon when she received the call. In a town where the police were usually called for disturbances or thefts, finding a dead body was an exceptional case. When she arrived at the dormitory, she was greeted by distraught staff. Their fixed gaze, trembling hands, and uncontrolled sobbing all pointed to a scene that had burned itself into the witnesses' memories.

Danielle lay lifeless on the floor of her room. Around her was a jumble of clothes, furniture, and personal belongings. A laundry basket covered parts of her body, and an overturned chair lay on top of her. It looked as if someone had tried to hide her—or bury her. Her T-shirt had ridden up, her face marked with bruises and traces of blood. A laptop cable was wrapped around her neck. A second cable, presumably from the stereo system, was also wrapped around her neck, and the tip of a mechanical pencil protruded from her mouth, thrust deep into her throat.

It was a crime scene that even experienced investigators rarely see. Excessive violence, almost staged. Signs of a struggle, an attack that testified to rage or deep hatred. It was clear: she was not a random victim. Someone had wanted to kill Danielle Davis and had done everything to make sure she didn't survive.

Danielle Davis had been a young woman full of life, ambition, and warmth. Growing up in Georgia, she was the center of her family from an early age. After the early death of her father, she took on responsibility, quickly growing into the role of the "little adult" and was, above all, one thing: reliable. She loved her mother, Stephanie, and her grandmother, Dale, dearly, two women she considered role models. When Stephanie fell ill, Danielle knew immediately that she wanted to study medicine. It wasn't just a degree program for her; it was a matter close to her heart.

She quickly settled in at Ogeechee Technical College. She lived in the dorms, took classes, worked part-time as a waitress, and enjoyed her newfound independence. Despite the stress of her studies, her part-time job, and her mother's illness, she managed to stay cheerful; her infectious laugh became her trademark. She found it easy to make friends. Men were also attracted to her, but Danielle remained reserved. For her, her education was the most important thing.

One of these men was Shane Allman, whom she had met while working in Savannah. Shane was older, charismatic, and seemed genuinely interested in her, but the relationship was complicated; distance, obligations, and mistrust made it difficult.

Danielle liked Shane, but she never let him get too close. Perhaps she sensed something she couldn't put into words.

Despite her many acquaintances, Danielle seemed to have no one who wanted to harm her. This made her death all the more puzzling for investigators. The police were under pressure. The night after the body was found, investigators began questioning people in the area. Friends laid flowers and lit candles in front of the dormitory. It was as if the whole city was holding its breath.

Among the mourners were two young men, Gerard Cook and Kurt Hyde. They were among the last people to see Danielle alive, and they volunteered to talk to the police. According to their statement, they had spent the evening before the murder with her. Together with a third friend, Darryl Priestly, they had visited Danielle to relax a little before their exams. Danielle had driven them to a remote parking lot to pick up Gerard's car, then they had driven back to her room. There they had sat, watched TV, and talked, nothing unusual, they said.

Around 10:30 p.m., they said goodbye, and Danielle was in a good mood. Gerard and Kurt said they went home afterwards, while Priestly drove to the library. They swore they had nothing to do with the murder, but their statements were difficult to verify—and the third important witness, Priestly, was suddenly unavailable.

The investigators were cautious, as voluntary statements did not necessarily mean innocence. They began to check every detail of the story: camera images, witnesses, and times. And they searched feverishly for Priestly, the last boyfriend.

Meanwhile, the preliminary coroner's report arrived and brought new details to light. Danielle had been brutally beaten, repeatedly in the face. Her lips were swollen, her ear was bleeding, and her eyes were bloodshot. The strangulation marks indicated a long struggle.

While these questions remained unanswered, investigators received DNA results from the crime scene. Skin cells had been found on one of the cables. It was a promising find. When DNA is secured on a strangulation tool, it is almost certain to come from the perpetrator. Now, only one thing was missing: a match in the database. Or a suspect who was willing to provide a voluntary sample. Suddenly, the case began to move forward.

While grief over Danielle Davis gripped the college, the police worked around the clock. The next few days were crucial, because most students would soon be leaving for the holidays. Every lead had to be followed up on, every conversation had to be had. Investigator Jake Wean, experienced and known for his tenacity, took charge. And it soon became clear that the story Gerard and Kurt had told was only part of the puzzle.

The third visitor, Darryl Priestly, remained missing. No one had seen him, no one could say where he was. His friends said he had gone to the library after meeting Danielle, but the cameras proved otherwise; he was not visible on any of the recordings.

When Priestly finally reported to the police voluntarily, the investigators were ready. The young man seemed calm, almost relaxed. At nearly two meters (almost 6.5 feet) tall and with a strong build, he was hard to miss, but his behavior was rather reserved. He spoke in a friendly but evasive manner. First, he said he had gone to the library to study. Then, when the investigators mentioned the recordings, he changed his story: he had only gone as far as the door, but had forgotten his USB stick, so he turned back.

These contradictory statements alone made him a suspect, but then a new detail came to light: a phone call. Shortly before she died, Danielle had called someone again. The number belonged to Darryl Priestly. Two short calls, right after the conversation with her boyfriend Shane. What did that mean?

Shane Allman had already been removed from the list of suspects at this point. His phone records, his location, his statements—everything matched his story. He was in Savannah at the time of the crime and could not have driven back to Statesboro without leaving a trace. But in his last conversation with Danielle, he had heard something: someone had knocked on her door. Danielle had said it was "Abby", but when investigators visited Abby Norris, it quickly became clear that she had nothing to do with the visit; she hadn't even been there. So, Danielle had lied. But why?

Maybe she didn't want to tell Shane that someone else had visited her. Maybe it was someone whose presence could cause problems. Or maybe she didn't want to worry her boyfriend. The police suspected that the person at the door was Priestly and that the conversation with him might have ended in murder.

When Priestly appeared for questioning, the investigators confronted him with the phone records. At first, he showed no reaction, but then he said he had forgotten his cell phone at Danielle's and had gone back to get it. She had let him in, and together they had found the device on the couch between the cushions. Shortly afterwards, he had left. Nothing more.

But this version didn't add up. It contradicted his earlier statement, and it didn't explain why Danielle was dead afterwards. The investigators believed that Priestly hadn't just gone back to get his cell phone. He had created an excuse to come back to be alone with Danielle, and something had escalated. Then came the decisive confession.

Under pressure, confronted with evidence, Priestly testified that Danielle had fallen, allegedly while playing around. In the process, the pencil had gotten stuck in her throat, she had swallowed it, and suffocated. It sounded like a lame excuse. The forensic examination clearly showed that the pencil had been inserted after her death. The strangulation marks told a different story as well.

What began as a clumsy attempt to portray his crime as an accident developed into a clear picture: Priestly had strangled Danielle with his bare hands and then with cables. He then tried to cover up the crime using bizarre methods. The pencil, the mess in the room, the laundry basket; it was all staged. But he had made one crucial mistake: he had left traces behind, and the truth could no longer be suppressed.

On December 22, 2009, just two weeks after the murder of Danielle Davis, Darryl Priestly was arrested. The investigators had enough evidence, and DNA traces on the cable used to strangle Danielle matched his DNA. His changing stories, the mysterious nighttime visit, everything pointed to him. And above all: his own confession, which raised more questions than it answered.

The authorities presented the case to the district attorney. The charge was first-degree murder. Priestly pleaded guilty. Not out of remorse, but because he knew there was no defense left. Every attempt to talk his way out of it had failed. The chain of evidence was complete.

In the days after the murder, Priestly had given the impression that he was a harmless friend, but in reality, something had been building up inside him. Perhaps jealousy, perhaps rejection, perhaps an obsessive affection that turned into violence. Investigator Jake Wean was convinced: Priestly had desired Danielle, and when she rejected him, he lost control.

What exactly happened that night could only be reconstructed. Danielle had let Priestly in, presumably believing it was a harmless visit. Maybe she really wanted to help him find his cell phone. She certainly didn't know how close she was to death. Then an argument broke out, perhaps an unwanted advance. Danielle fought back, and that was the moment when the violence exploded.

The traces in the room told the rest of the story: the struggle, the assault, the strangulation with cables and hands, the perpetrator's desperate attempt to cover his tracks. The most bizarre act, the pencil in her throat, was interpreted by the police as an attempt to make the murder look like an accident. As if Danielle had fallen unhappily, as if it had been "unintentional", but it was planned. Perhaps not well thought out, but carried out with full intent.

On January 10, 2010, Darryl Priestly stood trial. The prosecution demanded a life sentence without the possibility of early release. The court agreed with the request. Priestly showed little emotion during the trial. No tears, no explanations. Just a brief, barely audible admission of guilt.

It was no consolation to Danielle's family, but it was justice. Their daughter was dead, brutally killed by someone she knew and trusted, but at least her loved ones could be sure that this man would never be free again.

The small town of Statesboro was shaken. Vigils were still being held on campus, and the dorm room where it all happened remained empty. Danielle Davis became a memory that many could not let go of. Her story had become a symbol of the incomprehensible that can happen right in our midst.

The students who knew Priestly were shocked. For some, it was as if a stranger had been hiding behind the face of an acquaintance. For others, it was an oppressive feeling: the killer was not a stranger from outside. He was one of their friends.

For many, one question remained unanswered: Could it have been prevented?

Watch the video

A profiler's opinion on this case

CASE 9

9. DECEMBER

It was December 9, 2019, when a decision was made that marked the beginning of a deadly story. In an inconspicuous house in snowy Bismarck, North Dakota, two people sat together, bound by a secret darker than the long winter night outside. They were not lovers in the classic sense, not heroes, not victims.

They were a woman with a plan, and a man who was willing to kill for her. Nikki Entzel was 38 years old, a wife and mother of two, outwardly friendly, well-known in the community, polite, and committed.

But behind the façade, discontent was brewing. Her love for Chad Entzel, a quiet, reliable man, had long since grown cold. He worked in the energy sector, loved bowling, and rarely took center stage. Nikki Entzel, on the other hand, was looking for more: attention, adventure, and a way out.

She found that way out in Earl Howard, a man with a dubious past. The two met during an online training course. What began as a casual flirtation soon turned into an intense affair. Howard was charming, impulsive, and willing to do anything Entzel asked of him. And Entzel knew how to manipulate him.

On December 9, they decided together that Chad had to die. Not sometime, but soon. The details were still vague, but the goal was clear. Entzel said that she would "never be free as long as he was alive." Howard remained silent. He knew what that meant, and that there would be no turning back.

What they didn't realize that night was that every step they took would later be meticulously reconstructed. Every conversation, every shared glance, every message would be used against them. But at that moment, they felt safe. Untouchable.

In the days after the decision, they began their preparations. Entzel moved into a hotel room. She explained that the house was too cold. Chad stayed behind alone, unaware that his wife was no longer his wife. That she had already said goodbye in her mind. And that their love would not end in tears, but in fire.

On December 30, 2019, at 5:05 a.m., an emergency call came in. There was a fire on Burlington Drive. A single-family home, flames on the ground floor. When the fire department arrived, the men were met with a horrific scene: charred furniture, thick smoke, and a lifeless body in the back of the house.

The police were called in immediately, and it quickly became clear that this was no ordinary fire.

It took the fire department almost two hours to bring the flames under control. After the smoke had cleared, a scene of destruction remained: charred walls, a blackened ceiling, the typical smell of burnt plastic and wood, and a body discovered in one of the back rooms. The body was partially burned, lying on its back, and barely identifiable, but initial investigations quickly revealed that it was Chad Entzel, 42 years old, a resident of the house.

But something was wrong. The position of the body, the extent of the burns, and the condition of the furniture all indicated that the fire had not been the cause of death. Even before the autopsy was performed, the firefighters were certain that the fire had been set deliberately.

When forensic investigators examined the room, they found suspicious evidence: several cigarettes were scattered around the living room, and a portable fan heater had been positioned in close proximity to flammable materials. In the kitchen, there were open bottles of liquor, arranged in such a way that it looked staged, and the smoke detectors had been removed.

The investigators became suspicious. Why would Chad Entzel, who was known for his tidiness and reserve, leave cigarettes lying around, drink alcohol, and position heating devices in such a dangerous way? It didn't fit the picture, and it certainly didn't fit his usual lifestyle.

The police tried to contact Nikki Entzel. She called back in the late afternoon from a hotel in another part of town. Her voice sounded calm, almost too calm. She said she needed a few days' distance, that there had been an argument. That she knew nothing about the fire and only found out about it through a phone call.

But when she later came to the police, her answers seemed mechanical. She repeated several times that her husband had been acting strangely lately, that he had been going through depressive phases.

The investigators noted: no tears, no emotions, no questions about the condition of the house or the circumstances of the death. Nikki Entzel seemed distant and cold.

Initial suspicions began to form. Nothing had been proven yet, but one thing was clear: this fire was no accident, and Chad Entzel had not simply died in his sleep. Someone had killed him, and the fire was just a smokescreen to hide the truth.

On December 31, Chad Entzel's body was autopsied at the Bismarck Medical Examiner's Office. The forensic results left no room for doubt: two gunshot wounds—one in the back, one in the head. Both fatal. And there was another crucial piece of evidence: no soot was found in his lungs. This meant that Chad was already dead when the fire broke out.

With this finding, the case finally changed from a suspicious fire to premeditated murder. The staging as an accident or even suicide had failed; instead, there was now suspicion that someone had deliberately tried to destroy evidence. And the list of people with access to the house was short.

The investigators focused their attention once again on Nikki Entzel. She had made contradictory statements, had not been in the house on the night of the crime, and had behaved conspicuously calmly. When she appeared for further questioning, she suddenly told a new version of events: Chad had recently had alcohol problems. He had been unpredictable. She had been afraid. That was why she had withdrawn.

This explanation did not match the statements of former acquaintances or colleagues. Chad was considered reliable, calm, and never aggressive. There were no police calls, no known incidents of domestic violence. The new account seemed contrived—an attempt to hide a motive.

Then the investigators came across a name that Entzel had not mentioned before: Earl Howard.

A package in the house was addressed to him. What's more, the hotel room where Entzel had been staying for several days had been rented by him. And their credit card statements showed joint payments. It quickly became clear that the two were more than just acquaintances.

Entzel was confronted with the discovery. At first, she denied knowing Earl Howard. Then she admitted that yes, they had had an affair, but Chad had known about it. It had all been "complicated."

For the investigators, this was more than just a fling. It was a possible motive for the crime, and perhaps the decisive clue to a second perpetrator. Because if Entzel was not alone, if she was lying, then Earl Howard could be the key to the truth.

On January 1, 2020, an arrest warrant was issued for Howard, but the man had disappeared.

Earl Howard was arrested on January 2, 2020, in the small town of South St. Paul, Minnesota, after a search lasting several hours and an anonymous tip. He had been staying at a motel, apparently alone. In his luggage: clothes, cash, a cell phone, and a note with a list of things that "still needed to be done." One of the items on the list was "calm Entzel."

During the initial interrogation, Howard was calm, composed, downright sober. He did not outright deny the crime, but he was evasive. He only said he wanted to speak to a lawyer. But what he didn't know was that investigators had long since accessed his cell phone and location data. And this clearly showed that on the evening of December 29, Howard had been in a vehicle near the Entzel's house. He had been there several times, and, even more significantly, he was there on the night of the fire.

At the same time, Nikki Entzel was summoned again. Now, confronted with the location data and hotel bookings, she came under pressure. She changed her statement again. Now she claimed that she had not asked Howard to do anything; on the contrary, she had been shocked when she found out that Chad was dead. But this version did not hold up for long either.

Because Howard started talking.

In a comprehensive confession, he admitted to having planned the murder together with Entzel. Days earlier, they had discussed ways to "get Chad out of the way." Entzel had told him that Chad was violent and that she needed to protect herself. In his confession, however, Howard denied having fired the fatal shot himself. Entzel had called him and told him to come. When he arrived, Chad was already dead—that was his version of events.

But there were many indications that he knew more than he was admitting. He knew details about the crime scene that had not been made public. He talked about the placement of the cigarettes, the fan heater, the sequence of events that night, things that only someone involved could know.

The investigators were now faced with a classic dilemma: two perpetrators, two versions. Both shifted the responsibility onto each other, but one thing was clear: they were jointly responsible, and each of their contradictions tightened the noose.

On January 3, both Entzel and Howard were charged with second-degree murder, arson, and destruction of evidence. Their story, a story of affair, manipulation, and murder, was now being unraveled piece by piece.

With the double indictment of Nikki Entzel and Earl Howard, public attention began to grow rapidly. The local press, as well as national media, now followed the case daily. Because what was emerging here was more than a marital drama, it was a calculated murder with cold-blooded planning, committed by a woman who had previously been considered a caring mother and wife.

In the weeks that followed, investigators analyzed hundreds of messages exchanged between Entzel and Howard. These included chat histories, voice messages, and emails. The tone was clear: this was not just about love or an affair, it was about control, money, and a new life. In several messages, Entzel talked about wanting to be "free at last." That Chad was 'blocking' her. That she "deserved everything" he had.

Particularly damning was a message sent two days before the murder: "We can do this. After that, we'll be together. Forever."

While Earl Howard cooperated during his pretrial detention and repeatedly tried to portray himself as a follower, Entzel behaved completely differently. In prison, she was considered calm, almost demonstratively composed. She avoided other inmates, wrote notes, and appeared focused. Her lawyers began to build a defense strategy based on psychological stress and domestic violence.

An official later said, "She didn't seem like a woman who was afraid. She seemed like someone who wanted to stay in control."

The public reaction was divided. Some thought it was conceivable that Entzel had acted under pressure. Others saw her as a master manipulator. Online forums speculated whether she had unconsciously used Howard or whether she had deliberately pulled the strings and was prepared to drop him if necessary.

When the trial was scheduled to begin in 2022, it was clear that this case would not be easy. Not only the crime itself, but also the personality profiles of the perpetrators would be the focus of attention.

The trial against Nikki Entzel began in the spring of 2022 in the Burleigh County District Court. The prosecution presented a complete picture: joint planning, emotional and financial motives, manipulative communication, and a deliberate staging to make the murder look like an accident or suicide. It was not a crime of passion. It was cold and systematic.

During the trial, Earl Howard testified against Entzel again. He described in detail the conversations they had, Entzel's instructions, and her reaction after the murder. He admitted to setting the fire at her request, "to make everything disappear." Nikki Entzel, on the other hand, insisted that she had not been there, knew nothing about it, and that Howard had acted alone.

A forensic scientist testified, "This was not a spontaneous act. This was a carefully planned crime scene."

Particularly striking was a video clip from the police interview in which Nikki Entzel said with a blank stare, "I just wanted it to be over."

At the end of the trial, Entzel was found guilty on all counts: second-degree murder, arson, and destruction of evidence. She was sentenced to life in prison with the possibility of parole after 36 years.

Earl Howard, who had cooperated fully, received 25 years in prison.

In its ruling, the court referred to a "dangerous duo" and a "despicable abuse of trust and intimacy."

For Chad and Nikki Entzel's children, a world in ruins remained. Their father was dead, their mother a convicted murderer. Their grandparents took custody. The school organized psychological help, and the community collected donations.

A former friend of Chad summed up the case in an interview: "He hadn't done anything to anyone. He just wanted to love. And be loved."

Watch the video

A profiler's opinion on this case

CASE 10

10. DECEMBER

On December 10, 2007, there was unusual unrest in the small town of Ludowici, Georgia, USA. Deborah Gail Moody's motor home was surrounded by yellow police tape, and her car was parked untouched at the side of the road. Officers searched the interior, but everything looked tidy, in perfect order, and almost sterile. No signs of a struggle, no broken objects, and nothing to indicate violence. It was as if the 42-year-old mother had simply left her home and vanished into thin air.

For her neighbors and friends, this was unimaginable. Ludowici is a place where everyone knows everyone else. A small town between Savannah and Fort Stewart, with a single traffic light, no industry, and no large businesses. A place where strangers stand out and changes are noticed immediately. The fact that a woman had disappeared without a trace shook the entire community.

Officials soon realized that the clues to solving the mystery were not to be found on December 10, but a few days earlier. Deborah's mother, Melanie, remembered their last conversation clearly: on the morning of December 4. As usual, she had called her daughter and asked her to call back as soon as she got home. Deborah had simply replied, "Okay." But that call never came.

When Melanie, worried, asked her brother Randy to check on Deborah, everything seemed normal at first glance. The trailer was tidy, and there were no signs of a crime. Outside, around the property, there was nothing unusual to be found. But the absence of the woman who was always reliable and spoke to her mother every day immediately gave rise to an uneasy feeling.

Deborah was a quiet, introverted person who loved living in seclusion. She had bought a trailer and lived on her uncle's sprawling property—a hundred acres of land surrounded by forest. There she sought peace and quiet, far away from the hustle and bustle. But this seclusion, which otherwise offered her security, made her disappearance even more mysterious. No one had seen anything, no one had heard anything.

When investigators searched the house on December 10, they finally came across a detail that alarmed them. Deborah's keys, credit cards, cash, and even her cell phone were still in her handbag, untouched. Everything a woman would take with her if she disappeared voluntarily had been left behind. At that moment, it was clear to the police: Deborah had not simply walked away; something terrible must have happened.

Investigators focused on Deborah Gail Moody's last known movements. On the morning of December 4, she had started her shift as usual at the construction company in Fort Stewart, where she worked. She was considered reliable and conscientious. Nothing on that day indicated anything unusual.

Her supervisor, Rick Dennis, later recalled a small detail: After work, Deborah wanted to drive a colleague home, 42-year-old Gerald Brancham. It was nothing new for Deborah to help others, but this time it would be the last moment she was seen alive.

The next day, Gerald showed up for work as usual. Deborah, however, was missing. For everyone who knew her, this was a worrying sign because she was not the kind of woman who would be absent without excuse. In the days that followed, investigators sought to talk to Gerald, but even then, the first contradictions began to emerge. His boss had fired him shortly after Deborah's disappearance, but he did not give any clear reasons for doing so.

When the police checked his address, it turned out that Gerald had disappeared. A neighbor reported that he had packed his things and left in a hurry. For the officers, this was a clear warning sign. They immediately decided to find him.

In order to bring the man in for questioning, they asked his former supervisor for help. They contacted Gerald under the pretext that he could pick up his severance pay. Gerald agreed and actually showed up. Investigator Ty Smith addressed him directly: "We need to talk."

Gerald appeared calm on the outside. "I have nothing to hide," he explained. He confirmed that Deborah had driven him home. After that, he said he hadn't seen her again. His cell phone had been lost, so no one had been able to reach him, but Smith remained suspicious. The story sounded rehearsed, too smooth. The investigator was convinced: Gerald was hiding something.

To verify his alibi, Smith let him go for the time being. But no sooner had he returned to the office than he received a call that dispelled his suspicions. It was Deborah's friend Lyn Anderson. She reported that she had seen Deborah on that very evening, after she had dropped Gerald off. Together, they had bought a dog cage and later brought it to Deborah's trailer.

This made it clear that Gerald could not have been the last person to see Deborah. The lead that had seemed so suspicious just a moment ago led nowhere. The investigators had to start their search all over again, and the mystery surrounding Deborah grew even greater.

After the investigators had to drop the lead on Gerald Brancham, they turned their attention to Deborah's closest circle. Experience shows that family members or partners often play a role in missing person cases.

Deborah had close friends, Laurie Arrowood and Shelly Lumpkin, with whom she spent time regularly. In conversations with them, a picture emerged of a woman who was under personal stress. Her failed marriage in particular came into focus.

Jeff Moody had been her second husband. The two had known each other for years, and their families were close. They married in 2004, and at first, everything seemed stable, but it soon became apparent that Jeff was unable to take responsibility. While Deborah juggled her job, household, and raising the children, Jeff remained immature. She had to keep things in order, cook, drive his children to school, and work on top of that. Instead of being a partner, he became a burden to her.

In May 2006, Deborah acted: she filed for divorce and moved out of their shared home. By this time, Jeff had already started a new relationship. It was a profound change for Deborah, and tensions escalated. In a small town like Ludowici, such stories do not remain hidden; rumors spread quickly.

Jeff was an obvious suspect for investigators. After all, Deborah had taken out a life insurance policy that named him as the beneficiary. Could financial greed be a motive? However, it soon became clear that the sum involved was only a small amount, just two to three hundred dollars. Hardly a reason for such a drastic crime.

Jeff himself remained calm and cooperative during questioning. He insisted he had nothing to do with his ex-wife's disappearance. His presence at a National Guard exercise on the day of Deborah's disappearance was confirmed. This seemed to be another dead end.

For investigator Ty Smith and his colleagues, this meant another dead end. Time was running out, and with each day that Deborah was not found, the hope of bringing her back alive diminished.

As the days passed, investigators intensified their search for Deborah. The rural area around the trailer was vast, densely wooded, and difficult to access. Only one country road ran through it, lined with bushes and trees. Police combed the area, used dogs, and even requested the assistance of a helicopter. They searched hundreds of acres of land from the air without success.

The community of Ludowici also mobilized. Friends and relatives distributed flyers, collected donations for a reward, and held evening candlelight vigils. Billboards displayed a photo of Deborah, smiling and full of life. Everyone who saw it wondered if they could help. The town stood together and yet remained at a loss.

Weeks passed, and then, in January 2008, another woman disappeared in Georgia: Meredith Emerson, a 24-year-old student. Her case was quickly solved. Gary Michael Hilton, a 61-year-old serial killer who abducted and killed women in remote areas, was arrested. Hilton confessed to Emerson's murder and was soon linked to other crimes.

For Deborah's family, this came as a shock, and at the same time, it was a cruel case of déjà vu. Deborah had also disappeared in a lonely area, just a few miles from her neighbors. Could Hilton also be her killer? The circumstances seemed similar, but without evidence, this connection remained mere speculation.

The case stagnated until a surprising twist came months later.

In August 2008, an inmate from Liberty County came forward. He told investigators that his former cellmate had confessed to the murder of Deborah Moody. The name of this man: Marvin Jeffs.

Marvin was already known to the authorities for theft, drug crimes, and numerous minor offenses. He was a typical repeat offender who oscillated between prison and freedom. And he had indeed had contact with Deborah, as a plumber who had carried out repairs on her trailer several times.

Friends reported that Marvin had openly bragged about Deborah's disappearance. At parties, he allegedly said that he had raped and killed her. Sometimes he made insinuations, threatening women with the words, "Otherwise, you'll end up like the one who disappeared."

For investigators, this was a turning point. Many of his acquaintances independently confirmed that he had made such confessions. Everything pointed to Marvin knowing more than he was admitting, but as long as there was no evidence, it remained a suspicion.

The clues pointing to Marvin Jeffs initially seemed to be the breakthrough. Investigator Ty Smith arranged a meeting to question him. Marvin actually showed up, and his behavior was immediately noticeable: he avoided eye contact, stared at the floor, and tapped his foot nervously. When asked about Deborah, he gave evasive answers. He claimed to have barely known her and denied any connection to her disappearance.

When Smith increased the pressure, Marvin withdrew. He said he didn't want to say anything more. Finally, the investigator was persuaded to compromise: Marvin would voluntarily take a lie detector test. Surprisingly, he agreed, but when he saw Smith the next day, he suddenly refused to get into his car. He only showed up at a later appointment, but the results were inconclusive. It later emerged that he had taken sleeping pills the night before, which could have skewed the test results.

A third test finally produced a striking result: his reaction to a crucial question deviated from the norm. Nevertheless, this was not enough to bring charges. For the investigators, it was a frustrating game: hints, contradictions, but no solid evidence.

They entered Marvin's house with a search warrant. Rumors said he had recorded videos of himself abusing women. Perhaps there was material there that concerned Deborah. But the search was unsuccessful. Marvin later mocked the police and boasted that they would never find anything.

For weeks, the officers followed up on leads. They were told that Marvin had hidden Deborah's body under a concrete slab. Forensic scientists searched the area with special equipment designed to reveal features underground, but this lead also came to nothing.

In the end, all that remained were rumors, insinuations, and empty words. Marvin Jeffs was a man who liked to make himself important, who wanted to impress people with his stories. No one could prove that he was really involved in Deborah's disappearance. It was a bitter setback for the investigators. Once again, they found themselves at a dead end.

Almost three years after Deborah Moody's disappearance, the same district was shaken by another tragedy.

On September 25, 2010, Laurie Arrowood, 42, disappeared from her home in Long County. Her car was parked outside, her personal belongings were untouched; the scenario was a painful reminder of Deborah.

Laurie was no stranger to Deborah; on the contrary, the two women were friends, often went horseback riding together, and spent time with each other. The fact that Laurie had now also disappeared led the police to immediately draw parallels. Two women, almost the same age, both from the same area, both with similar appearances; it couldn't be a coincidence.

The investigation quickly led to a man from their immediate circle: Kenneth Lumpkin, Laurie's neighbor and family friend. He had been doing work at her house on the day she disappeared. When the officers questioned him, he appeared nervous. Finally, he broke down and confessed: he had killed Laurie.

This took the case in an unexpected turn. Lumpkin, himself a husband and father, had not only murdered a friend of the family but had also participated in the search for her while knowing the truth. For the investigators, this was almost inconceivable.

They immediately remembered the case of Deborah Moody. Lumpkin was her neighbor; they had been friends, and she had disappeared years earlier. Lumpkin initially responded dismissively to cautious questions. He insisted he had nothing to do with Deborah's disappearance, but the pressure remained.

In 2013, he finally pleaded guilty to the murder of Laurie Arrowood and was sentenced to life in prison. For a long time, he refused to say anything about Deborah. For her family, this meant agonizing years of uncertainty.

It was not until more than a decade after her disappearance, in 2019, that the truth finally came to light. Lumpkin accepted an offer: in exchange for information about Deborah, he would not receive a harsher sentence. He read the document, put it aside, and said, "Okay, I'm ready."

Then he described what had happened on December 4, 2007. Under the pretext of discussing Christmas presents, he had gone to Deborah's trailer. There, he had tried to rape her, but failed. Finally, he had dragged her into the trunk of his car, taken her to his parents' empty house, and tried again to abuse her. Again, without success. In his statement, he finally confessed that he had strangled her and disposed of her body in the woods.

Despite multiple search operations at the locations mentioned by Lumpkin, Deborah Moody's remains have not been found to this day. Officially, the case has been considered solved since 2019, even though the family never had the opportunity to bury Deborah.

Lumpkin continues to serve his life sentence in a Georgia prison. For the relatives, his confession was confirmation of the truth, but also a bitter realization: in this case, justice means the conviction of the perpetrator, but they are still denied a final farewell to Deborah.

Watch the video

A profiler's opinion on this case

CASE 11

11. DECEMBER

On December 11, 2023, everything seemed normal to outsiders. Lauren Johansen and her boyfriend, Bricen Rivers, were sitting in a bar in Nashville, having a drink and watching a football game. No one could have guessed that this evening would be the beginning of a nightmare. Just hours later, Lauren would be lying seriously injured and helpless in a car, and Rivers would be arrested for assault. It was the beginning of a tragedy that ended fatally months later.

Lauren was born on October 30, 2001, in Ocean Springs, Mississippi, a quiet coastal town with oak-lined streets, old houses, and ocean views. For tourists, it was a resort; for Lauren, it was home. She grew up with two older sisters, both of whom had health issues. Lauren learned responsibility early on, helping her parents with their care and developing a deep compassion for those who were weaker than herself.

Her love for animals was evident even as a child. Whether it was a dog, a cat, or an injured bird, Lauren cared for every living creature. Later, she regularly volunteered at the animal shelter and dreamed of one day founding her own rescue center. At the same time, she developed a desire to become a nurse, a profession in which she could help people in the same way.

In high school, she met Rivers, who was popular, athletic, and ambitious. At first, their relationship seemed harmonious, but soon the first warning signs appeared. Rivers became controlling, jealous, and manipulative. Friends noticed that Lauren was changing; she became quieter, canceled meetings, and made excuses, but she stayed with him. Out of fear? Out of hope? Out of love?

Outwardly, Lauren remained the helpful, friendly young woman who loved animals and stood up for others. But those around her noticed that she was changing. She canceled appointments more often, evaded questions about Rivers, and defended his behavior, even though it was obviously hurting her. Her friends were worried, but every time they brought it up, Lauren reassured them. She said Rivers was just stressed and needed her support right now.

Over time, his controlling behavior intensified. He wanted to know who she was talking to, what she had been doing all day, and wanted to dictate how she dressed. He kept a close eye on all her encounters with other men; even harmless words were viewed with suspicion. His jealousy toward male classmates or colleagues was particularly noticeable. Lauren began to withdraw increasingly to avoid conflict.

Rivers knew how to make her feel guilty. When Lauren tried to set boundaries, he portrayed her as cold or ungrateful. He said he loved her and only wanted what was best for her, but his love was full of conditions. Her emotional dependence grew. Rivers alternated between declarations of love and accusations, between tenderness and control. It became difficult for Lauren to recognize reality.

One day, after an argument, Rivers grabbed Lauren by the arm, firmly, roughly, frighteningly; it was the first time he had physically assaulted her, but she played it down. She told her friend that it had been a misunderstanding, that he hadn't meant it. It had just been a moment of overwhelm. She justified his behavior and stayed with him.

Her father, Robert, also noticed the change. He tried to talk to Lauren, but she shut him down. She told him to trust her, that everything was fine, but Robert had a bad feeling. He sensed that Rivers was not who he claimed to be.

The trip to Nashville in December 2023 was supposed to be a break for both of them. Rivers was on leave from the military for a few days, and Lauren was on vacation. They wanted to spend time together, visit sights, and get away from everyday life. But beneath the surface, things were simmering. The tension was palpable, even though Lauren tried to cover it up.

On the evening of December 11, 2023, Lauren and Rivers went to a bar in Nashville. Rivers was determined to watch an important football game, and Lauren accompanied him, even though she seemed tired. At first, everything seemed calm—they sat at a small table, ordered drinks, and talked quietly. Lauren smiled, but her eyes looked exhausted.

When she briefly went to the restroom and asked a waiter a question, things began to escalate. Rivers watched the scene with growing suspicion. As soon as Lauren returned, he accused her of deliberately flirting with the waiter. He raised his voice and accused her of infidelity out of nowhere. Lauren tried to calm him down, but Rivers became increasingly louder. Guests in the bar began to turn around.

The couple left the restaurant shortly afterwards. The argument continued in the car. Rivers locked the doors and took Lauren's cell phone so she couldn't contact anyone. His anger boiled over. He yelled at her, insulted her, and finally hit her.

Lauren fought back, tried to escape, banged on the windows, honked the horn, but there was no one around who could help. Rivers drove off to a remote area. He ignored Lauren's pleas and threatened to kill her. The situation escalated further in a deserted parking lot.

Lauren tried to reach into her bag, where she carried a small can of pepper spray, but Rivers snatched the bag from her. His brutality was indescribable.

In the middle of the attack, Rivers received a call from his mother. Lauren seized the moment and screamed for help. The mother immediately recognized the seriousness of the situation and alerted the police, even though she did not know where her son was. When the police contacted Lauren's father, Robert, he was able to tell them the current location of Lauren's cell phone thanks to a family app.

When the police found the vehicle, they heard Lauren's screams. They immediately opened the door. Lauren was seriously injured, her face covered in bruises. Rivers sat next to her, motionless. He was arrested at the scene, and Lauren was taken to the hospital.

Lauren received immediate medical attention. Her injuries were severe: bruises, hematomas, a bloodshot eye, scratches on her neck, and bruised ribs. She could barely speak. Nevertheless, she initially refused to press charges against him. She told the police that she didn't want to ruin Rivers' future; he was just going through "a difficult phase."

In prison, Rivers continued to try to influence her. Despite a restraining order, he called her indirectly. He promised to change, asked for forgiveness, and begged her not to press charges. Lauren, emotionally exhausted and deeply unsettled, finally agreed. She weakened her statement—a move that decisively changed the proceedings against Rivers.

The original charges were not immediately pursued. Although there was an audio recording of his conversation with his mother, medical reports, and witness statements, Rivers was released on $250,000 bail. Lauren's family was shocked; they knew what he was capable of.

A few months later, the bail was even reduced to $150,000; Rivers' mother paid it. He was allowed to return to Nashville with an electronic ankle bracelet. In theory, the device was supposed to monitor him, but serious errors occurred.

An official responsible for fitting the ankle bracelet had not been informed of the strict conditions. Rivers himself claimed that he was allowed to move freely around the city. No one checked the information, so the ankle monitor was configured incorrectly. Important restrictions on movement, such as the ban on contact with Lauren, were not considered.

Shortly afterwards, the device stopped charging, warning signals were ignored, and no one informed the police. Rivers' trail was lost, and no one reacted.

Lauren's father only received an automated voice message days later: the device was offline, and Rivers' whereabouts were unknown. This came as a shock to Robert Johansen. He knew his daughter was in danger, and this time, no one would be able to intervene in time.

On July 2, 2024, Rivers was officially reported as a fugitive, but by that time, he had already disappeared; his ankle monitor had not sent a signal for days. The police reacted late. Much too late.

On the morning of July 3, Robert tried again to reach Lauren without success. Instead, he received a text message from her number. The content was unusual: cold, distant, not in his daughter's tone. Robert knew immediately that she hadn't written this message.

Alarmed, he called Lauren's sister, with whom she lived.

The sister noticed that the apartment door was open, and Lauren's car was gone. The surveillance cameras in the driveway had been turned off, and everything pointed to something terrible having happened. Robert immediately reported his daughter missing, but even though there were now concrete indications of a dangerous situation, the police response was delayed again.

It was more than 24 hours before an active search for Lauren's vehicle began.

Meanwhile, the family tried to take matters into their own hands. With the help of a tracking app, they finally managed to locate Lauren's car. It was parked in a deserted parking lot near an old cemetery, isolated, surrounded by dense forest.

When the police and Robert arrived at the location, a man suddenly ran out of the car and disappeared into the woods: it was Bricen Rivers. An immediate chase was unsuccessful; the terrain was too confusing, and Rivers escaped into the darkness of the forest.

Robert, driven by the worst feeling, opened the car door. Lauren's lifeless body lay in the back seat, wrapped in garbage bags and a blanket. Her face was so badly disfigured that even her father could hardly recognize her.

The police immediately began securing the crime scene. Traces of blood in the vehicle indicated a brutal struggle. Everything pointed to Lauren having been severely abused in the car before she died.

That same night, a large-scale search for Rivers began. Emergency services combed the surrounding area with helicopters, search dogs, and thermal imaging cameras. Nine hours later, he was discovered deep in the forest. The officers surrounded him, and Rivers allowed himself to be arrested without resistance. His expression remained cold. No remorse. No emotion.

After his arrest, Rivers made a disturbing confession. He stated that he had intercepted Lauren early in the morning of July 3 as she left the house alone. He knew that she no longer wanted any contact with him, and that was precisely what drove him crazy.

He waited near her apartment. When she arrived, he approached her and confronted her. When she tried to avoid him, he grabbed her roughly and dragged her into the car. Inside, he locked the doors and drove off. His goal was to "finally have a clarifying conversation." But instead, an argument escalated. Lauren insulted him and threatened to go to the police again, and that's when he lost control.

First, he yelled at her, then he hit her. Again and again. At some point, she lost consciousness. Rivers claimed that he tried to revive her, but when she remained motionless, he decided to hide her in the hope of being able to take care of the "traces" later.

His statement was peppered with contradictory statements and derogatory remarks about Lauren. He spoke of "her fault", "her arrogance", and how she had "provoked" him. Not once did he mention grief; there was no remorse.

Meanwhile, the public was horrified. Not only by the crime itself, but also by the failure of the system. How was it possible that a man facing such serious charges was ever released? Why was the GPS ankle monitor not monitored correctly? Why was Lauren's family not warned in time? The sharpest criticism was directed at a judge who had significantly reduced the bail.

These questions now dominated the headlines. The judicial system came under massive pressure. Lauren's parents demanded a comprehensive investigation, gave interviews, and repeatedly emphasized that their daughter could still be alive if the system had worked.

The funeral service took place a few days later in Ocean Springs. Hundreds of people attended. Friends, neighbors, fellow students—even strangers who were deeply moved by Lauren's fate. The many white flowers, candles, and photos created an image of her that kept alive the memory of a young woman who had been full of compassion and joie de vivre.

Even while Rivers' trial was still ongoing, the family established a foundation in Lauren's name. Its purpose is to support animal shelters, promote rescue operations, and give a voice to young women in difficult relationships. The first donations came in shortly after its establishment.

Bricen Rivers' trial had been set for June 25, 2025, but was pushed to March 3, 2026. The charges are first-degree (capital) murder, theft of a vehicle, and tampering with evidence. His defense announced that he would present "his version of events."

To date, the trial has not been concluded. Lauren's family is once again sitting in the waiting room of justice, day after day, staring at the man who killed their daughter and destroyed their lives. The public is following every twist and turn, but a verdict is still pending. And with each day that the trial drags on, anger grows toward a system that knows the rules but rarely protects in a timely manner.

Watch the video

A profiler's opinion on this case

CASE 12

12. DECEMBER

December 12, 2018, seemed like a normal day for Laura Luelmo. The 26-year-old teacher left her small house in the Andalusian village of El Campillo to drive to school as usual. She had only moved in a few days earlier, and it was a temporary position at the high school in Nerva, a town nine kilometers away. She liked her new surroundings and wanted to settle into the small community quickly, but this day was not to end like any other.

In the evening, she sent her boyfriend a final message. After that, all traces of her were lost. Laura was a vivacious young woman with big plans. Raised in Zamora, she had studied fine arts in Salamanca and spent some time in Mexico. There, she had enrolled at the Universidad Autónoma de Puebla and deepened her knowledge of the humanities.

Friends described her as open, intelligent, and sensitive—someone who found it easy to connect with others. After returning to Spain, she decided to become a teacher, her true calling. In Nerva, she was appreciated by students and colleagues alike. When she was offered a small apartment in El Campillo, she gratefully accepted the offer. She wanted to live closer to the school and focus fully on her teaching.

But during her first few days in El Campillo, she noticed something eerie. An older man, her immediate neighbor, seemed to be watching her every time she left the house or returned to it. He stood at his window or on his doorstep, staring at her, but said nothing. Laura told her boyfriend about these encounters, calling him "strange" and mentioning that she felt uncomfortable. On December 12, she wrote that she wanted to go for a walk to avoid the neighbor's prying eyes. However, it was very windy, so she didn't know if she should really go. That was the last message she sent.

When Laura didn't show up for class the next day, her colleagues immediately became alarmed. She was reliable and always arrived on time. A colleague who had helped her find the house tried to reach her by phone, in vain. Her family was also unable to contact her. Her father reported her missing to the police, and the Guardia Civil sent a patrol to El Campillo. With the help of the landlord, the officers gained access to Laura's house, but the interior looked normal. There were no signs of a break-in, no signs of a struggle, and no evidence of a planned departure.

While the officers were still on site, the neighbor approached. He was carrying a laundry basket and seemed to be observing the scene closely. When asked if he had seen Laura, he gave an evasive answer. He said he didn't even know who lived there. He had little contact with his neighbors. Nothing about his story seemed credible, but there was no concrete evidence to detain him. The officers noted his name: Bernardo Montoya.

What they didn't know at the time was that Bernardo Montoya was anything but an ordinary neighbor. He was born on October 13, 1968, in Catalonia, together with his twin brother Luciano, but grew up in Cartagena. Even as a child, he exhibited antisocial behavior. In elementary school, the brothers set fire to a classroom; as teenagers, they fought, bullied others, and provoked their teachers. Later, drugs, theft, and violent outbursts were added to the mix.

At the age of 22, Montoya began a criminal career that repeatedly landed him behind bars. In 1995, at the age of 27, he committed a particularly brutal murder: he killed a 72-year-old woman, Cecilia, who was supposed to testify against him. He broke into her bedroom, hid behind the door, and stabbed her six times in the neck. He was sentenced to 17 years and seven months in prison for this murder.

In prison, Montoya was considered a quiet, unremarkable inmate. That is why he was granted prison leave for the first time in 2008, a grave mistake. During those few days outside the prison walls, he attacked again: he threatened a woman with a knife and stabbed her. She survived. For this, he received an additional year in prison.

But even after this incident, he was granted parole again in 2009. This time, he fled. He remained in hiding for ten months before voluntarily returning. Again, he received an additional sentence. His prison term finally ended in 2015, but just a few months later, he was convicted again, this time for two robberies involving the use of force. In November 2018, he was released again, just three weeks before Laura Luelmo moved into the house across the street.

The police, who initially found no evidence of a crime when Laura disappeared, now began to investigate Bernardo Montoya more closely. In his statement, he had claimed not to know Laura, but neighbors reported that he had often watched her. The fact that he happened to appear with a laundry basket during the house search now also seemed suspicious.

The police still lacked direct evidence, but Montoya's past, his behavior, and his proximity to Laura's disappearance made him the prime suspect.

On the evening of December 13, one day after Laura's disappearance, Montoya suddenly fled his home. A neighbor observed him and reported it to the police. However, the officers were initially unable to apprehend him. The next day, he unexpectedly showed up at the hospital with an injury to his jaw. At the same time, he visited a former prison acquaintance. For the investigators, this was a clear sign that he was on the run but was also trying to establish an alibi.

The police intensified their search. Specialists were called in, and Laura's house was searched again, this time together with her father and her boyfriend. They confirmed that Laura's sports shoes, her pants, her cell phone, and her keys were missing. Everything pointed to something having happened to her on her walk.

No one yet knew the extent of this crime.

In the early morning of December 15, the search for Laura entered a new phase. Investigators analyzed the geodata from her cell phone for the first time. This showed that the last signal had been received at exactly 9:00 p.m. on December 12 via a transmission tower near El Campillo, close to her home. The police now knew that Laura had not gotten far; everything indicated that she had never left the neighborhood.

A large-scale search operation immediately began within a five-kilometer radius. Volunteers, sniffer dogs, and helicopters assisted the police. There was still no trace of Laura, and her belongings remained missing. Only her car stood untouched in front of the house. Suspicions against Bernardo Montoya continued to mount.

On December 16, the search was expanded to a radius of ten kilometers. Even more helpers and emergency personnel joined the effort. On that day, the search team came dangerously close to the crucial location, but she remained undiscovered, for the time being.

It was not until a day later, on December 17, at around 12:30 p.m., that a volunteer made a gruesome discovery in an open field. First, he found pieces of clothing. About two hundred meters away: the half-naked body of a woman. It was Laura. She could only be identified with certainty by a tattoo on her upper body.

Specialists from Madrid arrived by helicopter that same day. They secured evidence and examined the area. It quickly became clear that she could not have come to this place on her own. Someone must have transported her there. The questions were: when, how, and why?

On the night of December 18, the police stormed Montoya's house. The officers smashed a window and searched the entire building. What they found confirmed their worst suspicions. In the living room, they discovered several bloodstains, which later turned out to be Laura's blood.

Meanwhile, Montoya was being followed by the police on his return to El Campillo. When he realized he was being followed, he jumped out of his car and ran into a nearby wooded area, but his escape was short-lived. Just a few minutes later, he was apprehended, arrested, and taken to the police station.

An interrogation lasting several hours followed. Montoya remained silent for a long time, evaded questions, and tried to deny everything. But in the end, under the pressure of the evidence, he confessed to the murder and gave his version of how the crime allegedly took place. Others were to follow. He said that he had seen Laura on the day of her disappearance. That she had asked him for directions to the supermarket. That he had lured her into a trap, into a dead-end street, where he knocked her down and put her in the trunk of his car.

He said he hadn't raped her, but only undressed her. He claimed to have left her unconscious but alive, but even then, the investigators knew that this story couldn't be true; the evidence told the truth.

First, there was the blood. In the living room of his house, specialists found several blood spatters, clearly identified as Laura's DNA. Investigators also found other genetic traces that came from both him and the young teacher. This proved that she had not only been in his vicinity, but she had been in his house and had been injured there.

Added to this were the results of the forensic autopsy. Laura's body showed clear signs of sexual violence, and Bernardo Montoya's DNA was found on her. This meant that his claim that he had merely undressed her and then left her behind was no longer tenable. The estimated time of her death, which had initially remained unclear, was also specified after the autopsy: Laura had died on December 14 or 15. Montoya had probably left her seriously injured in the field to die.

The prosecution was convinced that Montoya had lured Laura into a trap under false pretenses, forced her into his house, raped her, and then brutally murdered her. Afterwards, as forensic evidence revealed, Montoya transported the body in his car and hid it in a remote location. To confuse investigators, he threw her clothes in a different location and disposed of her cell phone in the opposite direction. He was also able to be linked to the phone being turned off at around 9:00 p.m., exactly the time when the last signal was received.

Particularly disturbing was the cold-bloodedness with which Montoya proceeded. After committing the crime, he returned to his house, superficially removed the traces, washed himself, changed his clothes, as if nothing had happened. Later, he deliberately sought out places where he could be seen, as if he wanted to establish an alibi.

But not everything went according to plan. The police had their eye on him early on, albeit cautiously at first. It was only after his hasty escape and strange behavior that it became clear that something was wrong.

During a search of his home on December 18, investigators finally reached the point where they could no longer doubt their suspicions. Too many pieces of the puzzle fit together. Montoya's history also made it clear that he was not a random perpetrator. He had murdered a woman before, at that time, to prevent her from testifying against him in court. And even after his release, he had been involved in further acts of violence.

On December 19, 2021, the decisive turning point came. The trial took place in the provincial court of Huelva behind closed doors. The presiding judge had decided this.

The family did not want any further public display of their pain, no more headlines, no more sensational images on the evening news, and declared that they would no longer make any statements to the media.

The defense pursued a clear strategy. It continued to claim that Bernardo Montoya was not the perpetrator. Rather, another woman he had met in prison was responsible. Montoya himself had changed his story again and now claimed that he had only helped to transport the body. His motives? Love, drugs, confusion; that's how his lawyer explained it. The person in question had asked him for help, and he had been emotionally unable to say no.

But the trail to her led nowhere. When the police investigated the alleged location of the murder weapon, a hammer she was supposed to have used, they found nothing. The suspect herself was summoned as a witness, but did not appear at first. An arrest warrant was requested, but it later turned out that she had a watertight alibi. Nothing, neither evidence nor circumstances, linked her to Laura's murder.

The defense tried another argument: Montoya was medically impotent. A medical report was presented to the court to undermine the rape charge, but even that was not enough. The prosecution presented a detailed chronology of the crime based on forensic evidence, DNA traces, witness statements, and telephone records.

The reconstruction of events painted a clear picture: Montoya had acted deliberately. He wanted Laura for himself, and when she resisted, she became a threat. Afterwards, he desperately tried to cover his tracks. He hid the body, put her clothes away separately, threw away her cell phone, and cleaned his house. Everything he had done indicated that he was trying to buy time and mislead investigators.

It was a verdict that hardly anyone questioned; the evidence was too clear, the sequence of events too obvious.

But even after the verdict, a feeling of emptiness remained. Because no verdict could ever make up for what Laura's family, friends, and colleagues had lost. They had lost a loved one through the violence of a man who should never have been free.

On December 10, 2021, almost exactly three years after Laura's disappearance, the verdict was announced. Bernardo Montoya was sentenced to life imprisonment for murder. In addition, he received a further 17.5 years' imprisonment for deprivation of liberty in connection with a sexual offense. The fine was €400,000, as compensation for Laura's parents and siblings.

The verdict was an act of justice, but it offered no consolation. The relatives sat silently in the courtroom, holding hands. There was no cheering, no relief, just a moment of silence as the judge left the courtroom. It was a moment that spoke louder than any words.

In the days that followed, the verdict was discussed throughout Spain. Many spoke of a judicial scandal, not because of the decision, but because a man with so many previous convictions had been free in the first place. It was not the first time Bernardo Montoya had committed a crime. If he had been stopped earlier, Laura would still be alive. This question echoed through talk shows, newspapers, and political debates, but no one had an answer.

In El Campillo, silence fell. The small village that had become Laura's last home sank into a kind of collective mourning. No one talked about the case anymore, but everyone remembered. The place where her body had been found was never entered again. At the school where she had taught, her name remained on a hand-painted poster for a long time: "Laura, we will not forget you."

Her students were young, but they understood that something irretrievable had happened. The teachers tried to put it into words, but how do you explain to children that someone is no longer coming because someone else decided to take their life?

And every year, when December comes around, someone quietly places a white flower in front of the school where she taught. A silent gesture. A promise that she will not be forgotten.

Laura's family largely withdrew from public life. Only once, months later, did her father appear in front of a camera. With a broken voice, he said:

"My daughter had dreams, talents, love. And someone wiped all that away. I just hope that her name reminds us all how important it is to protect – before it's too late."

Watch the video

A profiler's opinion on this case

CASE 13

13. DECEMBER

On December 13, 1995, a manhunt came to an end. For weeks, police in several states had been searching for a murder suspect, but on that cold winter morning, a simple phone call changed everything. Kent Elmore, an acquaintance of the suspect, believed he had recognized him at a motel in California. Within hours, a SWAT team arrived. They surrounded the building, prepared for the worst, but Robert James Acremant surrendered without resistance. As he was led away, he was calm, almost relieved.

No one knew at that point how deep the abyss was that this man had opened behind him. The police only knew what they had learned from the news: two women murdered in Oregon, shots that appeared to be a targeted act of hatred, but when they questioned Acremant, he opened up, almost willingly. He talked a lot, as if he had been waiting for someone to finally listen, and what he had to say was even more terrifying than anyone had feared.

Robert James Acremant was born in 1968 and grew up in California. Early on, he was considered an intelligent student, but his interpersonal relationships remained difficult. At school, he was quiet, shy, and sometimes absent. Friends later described him as "socially awkward," someone who preferred computers to people. After high school, he studied business administration and worked at various companies, but never for long; it was as if he had never really found his place.

In the mid-1990s, it seemed as if he was on the verge of a financial breakthrough. He had invested in stocks and started a small business, but something went wrong. He lost money, and perhaps also control, and amid this unstable phase, he met a woman who would change everything: Roxanne Ellis.

What Acremant was thinking or feeling in the days before the murders can only be reconstructed today. The only thing that is certain is that on December 4, 1995, he lured Roxanne and her partner, Michelle Abdill, into a trap under false pretenses. A few days later, both women were found dead in the trunk of a car, shot with the same weapon.

The country was shocked: two women, openly lesbian, committed, popular in their community, and murdered in cold blood. At first, investigators were baffled. There were no signs of forced entry, no obvious motive. But now, with Acremant in custody, the picture began to clear up.

During questioning, Robert Acremant began to talk. And he hardly stopped. What the investigators heard sounded like the confused confession of a man who had long since lost himself. He talked about money problems, about humiliation, and about the desire to "be someone." Again and again, he returned to one topic: his relationship with a woman named Alla Kosova.

Alla was a sex worker from Las Vegas whom Acremant had visited regularly in the months before the murders. He spent thousands of dollars, booked luxurious hotel rooms, and bought expensive gifts. For him, Alla was more than just a sex worker; she was an obsession.

But when his money ran out, he lost contact with her.

Acremant felt betrayed, used. He began to spin a new story in his head: that he could only get his money back by pulling off a big coup, and that coup had a name: Roxanne Ellis. Roxanne worked as a real estate agent in Medford, Oregon, and was well known for her volunteer work in the queer community.

Michelle Abdill, her partner, supported her in everything. Together they lived openly, committedly, and visibly, which Acremant found provocative. A dangerous thought formed in his mind: if he kidnapped Roxanne, blackmailed her, or even killed her, he might be able to make a statement, or at least get money. It was a mixture of delusion, hatred, and greed.

On December 4, 1995, Acremant called Roxanne and pretended to be a potential buyer for a property. They met in the late afternoon to view the apartment, but instead of a business deal, violence awaited her: Acremant threatened her with a gun, tied her up, and forced her to call Michelle. She, too, was lured into the trap shortly thereafter. He took control of both women and drove them in Michelle's car to California, to his parents' house, which was empty at the time. There, in the garage, he held them captive overnight.

The next morning, he killed them with shots to the head at close range. With the bodies in the trunk, he drove to Medford, Oregon. He parked Michelle's car in the parking lot of the South Ashland Apartments. The vehicle was discovered days later, with the bodies of the two women inside.

The cold-blooded nature of this crime left even experienced investigators speechless. It was not a crime of passion, nor was it the result of an argument; it was planned, prepared, and carried out with clinical precision. The community was shocked.

For Acremant, however, it was not over. The next chapter was already beginning in his mind: the murder of Scott George, an old acquaintance from California.

After disposing of the women's bodies, Acremant did not stay long in Oregon. He drove back to California, where he stayed briefly with his mother in Walnut Creek, but the inner pressure continued to grow. He spoke of feelings of guilt, but also of the feeling that there was no way out. His worldview was fragile; reality had long since begun to crack. Acremant kept talking about "completing something." No one knew exactly what that meant until December 11.

On that day, he made plans to meet with Scott George, an old acquaintance from his college days. The two hadn't seen each other in years, but Acremant had specifically contacted him. In truth, it was not a harmless reunion; it was a trap. Scott George was gay, and in Acremant's confused mind, this became another reason for violence. He later said that Scott had "hit on" him, but this was never confirmed. It is more likely that Acremant had a clear goal in mind: to prove his dominance, to exercise control, perhaps also to suppress his own inner conflicts.

On the evening of December 11, he killed Scott George in his apartment in Visalia. Again, it was an execution, cold and deliberate. Acremant took some valuables and fled, but this time, he did not remain calm. It almost seemed as if he wanted to be caught.

Two days later, on December 13, 1995, a man named Kent Hensley saw an old acquaintance in a fast-food restaurant in Redding, California. He was certain: it was Robert Acremant. Kent knew about the wanted photos and had been following the news. He didn't hesitate and alerted the police, and Acremant was arrested.

In his car, investigators found the gun used to commit the murders, and in his pockets: a list of other names. Potential victims? No one knew for sure. There would probably have been more deaths if he hadn't been caught.

After his arrest on December 13, 1995, Robert James Acremant was remanded in custody in California. Investigators were faced with a man who initially appeared withdrawn but then became talkative. Within a few days, he not only confessed to the murders of Scott George and the lesbian couple in Medford, but also began explaining his motives. It was a harrowing insight into a disturbed mind.

Acremant spoke of voices in his head, of "missions" he had to carry out, but beneath this confused surface lay a crude ideology. He repeatedly emphasized that he felt "hatred toward homosexuals," especially men who reminded him of his own insecurity, and toward women who made him feel powerless.

During questioning, Acremant admitted that his actual goal had been much greater: he had planned to carry out a series of "purges," starting in California, then Oregon, and perhaps even further north. He had created lists of names of people he believed to be gay, lesbian, or simply "different." So, the murders of Roxanne and Michelle were no coincidence; they were part of a frightening plan that he himself described as "rational."

The investigators were faced with a dilemma. On the one hand, they were dealing with a serial killer who had confessed to his crimes. On the other hand, Acremant showed clear signs of mental disorder, but was he really insane? Or just manipulative? A psychiatric evaluation was ordered, and the experts concluded that Acremant probably suffered from narcissistic personality disorder and paranoid traits, but was criminally responsible. He knew what he was doing and why.

Meanwhile, the victims' families tried to come to terms with the incomprehensible. The relatives of Roxanne Ellis and Michelle Abdill became the focus of media attention. The two women were well known in Medford, active in the community, and politically engaged. Their deaths shook not only the town but the entire LGBTQ+ community far beyond. The public began to ask questions: could Acremant have been stopped earlier? Why was a repeatedly failed businessman with delusions capable of killing so cold-bloodedly?

In January 1996, Acremant was transferred to Oregon to stand trial for the double murder of Roxanne and Michelle. The prosecution sought the death penalty. For many, this was the only just punishment.

But the trial was not as straightforward as initially believed.

The trial of Robert James Acremant began in the fall of 1996 at the Jackson County Circuit Court in Medford, Oregon. Security measures were tight, and the public gallery was full. Members of the LGBTQ+ community had come out of grief, out of protest, out of a need for justice. The prosecution presented a man who had killed out of hatred, in his right mind, but with a deep abyss within him.

The prosecution described how Acremant had sought out his victims, deceived them, tied them up, intimidated them, and finally shot them in cold blood. It was an act, they argued, that was not only murder but a targeted attack on a minority. The murders were an expression of "deep-seated hatred" that had been unleashed in targeted violence.

The defense, on the other hand, painted a different picture. It attempted to show that its client was mentally ill, a man who had lost touch with reality, plagued by paranoid thoughts, voices in his head, and a distorted perception of reality. Acremant himself appeared different in the courtroom: sometimes calm and composed, then again erratic, with confused remarks that repeatedly brought the proceedings to a standstill.

A central theme was Acremant's relationship with his father, a conservative military veteran who despised any form of weakness. Acremant repeatedly emphasized that he had never been good enough, that he had felt he had to prove his masculinity in destructive ways. His experiences with sex workers and the rejection he had experienced there also seemed to reinforce his self-hatred.

But despite all attempts at explanation, the core of the crimes remained brutal. The jury listened to audio recordings of the interrogations in which Acremant spoke about his motives, with cool matter-of-factness. There was no sign of remorse, only the conviction that he had "set something right."

On October 9, 1996, the court announced its verdict: guilty on all counts. The jury recommended the death penalty. Judge Rebecca Orf confirmed the verdict, and Robert James Acremant was officially sentenced to death.

After his conviction, Acremant was transferred to Oregon's maximum security prison's death row. Although the verdict was clear, his case was far from over, because Acremant continued to talk. A lot. And with every new interview he gave, he cast himself in an even darker light.

In a letter to a local newspaper, he claimed to have killed more people, four, maybe five. He didn't name names or dates, just hints. Whether these confessions were true or the expression of a man who had lost all control remained unclear, but one thing was clear: his psyche was severely damaged.

Acremant's behavior became increasingly erratic. At times, he spoke of remorse, at others of pride. He complained about the death penalty, but did not want to appeal. "I want to die," he wrote to a reporter. "I have nothing left to give." At the same time, he tried to publicize his case in the hope of at least being heard as a voice against the system.

In prison, he was an isolated figure. Other inmates avoided him, and guards described him as unpredictable. His file continued to grow, not with legal proceedings, but with psychological assessments that spoke of severe personality disorders, narcissistic traits, and paranoid delusions.

Robert James Acremant died on October 19, 2018, at the age of 50, not by lethal injection, as originally planned, but of natural causes. He died alone in his cell, the same place where he had spent over two decades.

For many, it was a quiet end to a harrowing story. No new confessions, no last words. Just the bland end of a man who had found his way into history through hatred, despair, and self-destruction; as a perpetrator, as a symbol, as a warning.

Watch the video

A profiler's opinion on this case

CASE 14

14. DECEMBER

On December 14, 1991, a high school student disappeared without a trace in broad daylight, in the parking lot of her own school in Federal Way, near Seattle. Sarah Yarborough, sixteen years old, was a member of the Federal Way High School cheerleading team. That Saturday morning, the team was supposed to leave together for a competition, but Sarah was early; she had miscalculated the departure time and arrived an hour early. When her teammates arrived later, her car was in the parking lot, but there was no sign of Sarah.

Around 9 a.m., two twelve-year-old boys went to the school grounds to run around and explore. When they reached the wooded area behind the tennis courts, they saw a strange man stepping out of the bushes. He was tall, had long blond hair, and was wearing dark clothes. He glanced at them briefly and then walked in the opposite direction. The boys thought he was strange, but not dangerous, until they ventured a few meters further and came across something they would never forget.

A girl was lying motionless on the ground between the trees. Her clothes were partially dislodged, her face marked with dark spots and dirt. The boys were frightened, ran home, and informed their parents. While the father of one of them called 911, the other tried to follow the strange man.

His son told him that he had seen a vehicle that looked like a Chevrolet Nova driving away from the scene. Since he lived near the school, the father decided to drive out onto the road and try to find the car. Eventually, he managed to spot a similar vehicle, but it quickly disappeared, and the man was unable to find it again.

A short time later, police officers arrived at the scene, and it quickly became clear that the girl was dead. It was Sarah Yarborough. Investigators found her jacket, socks, and underwear near the body, and her wallet and car keys were still in her car.

The police secured the scene and immediately began their investigation. The cause of death was quickly determined: Sarah had been strangled with her own tights. In addition, the medical examiner found a severe head injury, which had probably caused her to lose consciousness before she was killed.

At about the same time as the boys, a jogger had noticed a man bent over a motionless girl, but he thought it was a couple who wanted to retreat into the woods; a misunderstanding that would later cause much discussion. He did not intervene, but later reported what he had seen to the police. His description also matched that of the children: a young man with long blond hair, in his early twenties, wearing dark clothing.

The investigators followed the initial leads. Particularly striking were the traces of male semen that were found on almost all the victim's clothing, clearly coming from a single person. However, there were no signs of a classic sexual assault. The forensic experts concluded that the perpetrator had probably committed lewd acts while the girl was unconscious or already dead. A DNA database, as it exists today, did not yet exist at that time. DNA could only be compared directly with samples from suspects, and so far, there had been no matches.

Investigators created a composite sketch of the suspect based on the statements of the children and the jogger. This image was distributed throughout the region. The public was shocked, and the murder was the talk of the entire state of Washington. The fact that a young girl had been murdered on school grounds, on a Saturday morning, without anyone intervening in time, left many people stunned.

The investigation was in full swing. Within a few days, officers had spoken to over seventy people who had been on or near the school grounds on the morning of December 14, 1991. Hundreds of tips were received by the police. The media reported on the murder daily, and the students at Federal Way High School lived in fear from then on. The girls avoided walking around the grounds alone. The boys from the football and track teams volunteered to accompany their female classmates to their cars or buses. The school tried to return to normal, but the shadow of the crime remained.

The police followed up on every tip; almost 4,000 over time. In one case, the description seemed to fit a man with a criminal record who matched the composite sketch, but his DNA did not match the evidence found at the scene. And that was the catch: as long as no suitable suspect could be found who was also willing to provide a DNA sample, the investigation could not proceed.

Sarah's grandfather, who worked for a large technology company, convinced his company to provide the police with a high-performance computer worth $150,000. In the 1990s, this was an enormous help: finally, all the clues could be stored centrally and evaluated efficiently. Despite this technical support, the investigation remained without a decisive breakthrough.

Two years later, Sarah's former classmates graduated. A memorial plaque was donated in their honor. It was intended not only to commemorate them but also to give hope that justice would one day prevail.

In the years that followed, the case was regularly reopened. Investigators repeatedly examined the old leads, repeatedly without success. The officers interviewed thousands of people and took nearly three hundred DNA samples, but none of them matched, and hope was fading. Then, twenty years after the murder, a new investigator had an idea: he wanted to use genetic genealogy, a method that was still new at the time, which could be used to identify perpetrators through their family relationships.

The investigator turned to a company that specialized in this field. The experts took on the case, but in 2011, the technology was still in its infancy. For example, it was not possible for them to find both male and female relatives with only one male DNA sample. In addition, legal regulations restricted the use of genetic data. Nevertheless, the investigators came across an interesting connection: the perpetrator was related to Robert Fuller, one of the passengers on the Mayflower, the famous ship that sailed from England to the New World in 1620.

This lead did not help, unfortunately, as there are around 25 million Americans descended from the few passengers who traveled on the ship. Finding a specific perpetrator among this large number seemed hopeless. The investigator found several men named Fuller who had lived in the region at the time of the crime and asked them for DNA samples. One was indeed a descendant of Robert Fuller, but not the murderer.

In 2017, the investigator retired, but the case was not shelved. A new team took over, with new methods and new databases. They contacted the genetic genealogy company again. And this time, with better technology and more comprehensive information, a picture finally began to emerge.

It took two years before the genetic data finally yielded a promising lead. The investigators analyzed publicly available family tree databases and were able to identify distant relatives of the perpetrator. Step by step, they reconstructed his family connections until they came across two brothers who were living in the Federal Way area at the time of the crime. One of them was Patrick Nicholas.

Nicholas was 27 years old at the time and already had a history of violent crime. He had been on record for multiple sexual assaults, including against minors. However, in the early 1990s, there was no mandatory DNA collection for offenders in this category. As a result, his DNA never appeared in the databases, and he was never suspected.

Investigators immediately began discreet surveillance. Nicholas was now living in the city of Wellington. They watched him around the clock, waiting for an opportunity to obtain a DNA sample. It came sooner than expected: in a laundromat, Nicholas carelessly threw a smoked cigarette on the floor. Shortly afterwards, he also lost a used tissue. The police secured both items.

The decisive evidence was found in the laboratory: Patrick Nicholas' DNA matched exactly with that found on Sarah's clothing in 1991. Within a few days, an arrest warrant was issued. Nicholas was arrested 28 years after the murder.

Patrick Nicholas was immediately charged.

At the age of nineteen, he approached a girl, got into her car, and attempted to sexually assault her, causing her to flee in panic. She saved herself by jumping into a river, and Nicholas served four years in prison for this. Later, in 1994, he was arrested again for attempting to rape an underage girl, but this time he was convicted under a statute that did not require DNA sampling. So, his genetic data never made it into the database. Investigators searched through thousands of leads, but his name never came up.

Decades later, the case finally moved forward, thanks to genetic genealogy. It turned out that Nicholas' grandfather had been adopted, which changed his surname, misleading investigators for a long time. Only when his name finally came up did one of the boys who had found Sarah's body at the time immediately recognize him. "It's him. I know for sure," he said. Finally, the witness felt certain.

The trial began in 2023. Nicholas maintained his innocence. His lawyer tried to challenge the validity of the DNA evidence without success. The experts declared that the match was clear. The traces on Sarah's clothes came from him.

On May 25, Patrick Nicholas was found guilty of first-degree murder. He was sentenced to 45 years and 8 months in prison, effectively life imprisonment. While Sarah's family tearfully thanked the court for the belated justice, Nicholas showed no emotion. He had remained undetected for twenty-eight years, but in the end, the truth had caught up with him.

Watch the video

A profiler's opinion on this case

CASE 15

15. DECEMBER

On December 15, 2020, the moment had arrived. In Tokyo, a verdict was handed down that shook the whole of Japan. An oppressive silence reigned in a small, heavily secured courtroom as the presiding judge announced the sentence: death penalty. The defendant, Takahiro Shiraishi, showed little reaction. He just nodded slightly, as if he had expected exactly this verdict. No flinching, no objection—just silent acceptance of his fate.

Shiraishi was no ordinary murderer. The media had long since dubbed him the "Twitter killer", a man who deliberately searched social networks for desperate, suicidal people. His promise was perfidious and simple: "I'll help you die." Nine young people (seven women and two men) believed him. They met with him, and every time, he kept his promise: those who needed psychological help during a difficult time got what they wanted.

On that cold December morning, Shiraishi finally became the symbol of a digital nightmare. In a world where likes, retweets, and private messages were part of everyday life, he used the same channels to find his victims. The brutality of his crimes was as shocking as their systematic planning.

The trial lasted only a few weeks. Shiraishi showed no remorse, confessed to every detail, did not contest any of the charges, and in the end even waived his right to appeal. Not out of guilt, but out of indifference. "I have no regrets – except that I was caught," he said. And with that sentence, it became clear: this was not a madman, but a calculating murderer.

But Shiraishi's story began long before the massacre in his apartment. It began in a quiet corner of Japanese society that often overlooked or suppressed mental suffering. That's exactly where the trail led back to, and that's exactly where the story that is now being told begins.

Takahiro Shiraishi was 27 years old when the police arrested him in October 2017. He lived alone in a small apartment in Zama, Kanagawa Prefecture, just a few kilometers from his parents' home. The apartment was unremarkable, functional, with an improvised curtain in front of the window and an old mattress on the floor. But behind this facade lay a nightmare that even experienced investigators had never seen before.

In several coolers covered with cat litter, officers discovered the remains of nine people, carefully dismembered, labeled, and stowed away. The air was filled with an almost unbearable smell of decay. A white bag containing personal items immediately revealed that one of the victims was Tamura Aiko, a young woman from Hachioji who had been missing since October 23.

The clue that led to the arrest had been found by her brother. Concerned about her sudden loss of contact, he had searched her social networks and found a disturbing chat history. Aiko had written about her suicidal thoughts in a forum: "I want to die, but not alone." Shiraishi had replied, kindly, sympathetically. He pretended to be an ally, someone who understood her pain. In reality, he had already prepared a location, procured tools, and planned his next murder.

For weeks, the police had been searching not only for Aiko, but also for other young people whose last signs of life could be traced back to the same online platforms. It was a puzzle of disappearances, mental instability, and digital traces, and all the threads ultimately led to Shiraishi's apartment.

Interviews with neighbors revealed little. Some remembered an unpleasant smell coming from the apartment. Others had considered him a quiet, polite young man who rarely had visitors. No one suspected that behind this silence lived a serial killer, someone who systematically led the most vulnerable members of society to their doom.

The discovery of the apartment sparked an investigation that not only shocked the public but also raised fundamental questions about mental health, social isolation, and the dark side of the internet.

The first confirmed victim of Takahiro Shiraishi was 21-year-old office worker Miura Mizuki from Atsugi. She suffered from mental health issues that originated from years of bullying during her school days. She searched social networks for like-minded people, people who, like her, were toying with the idea of suicide. That's how she met Shiraishi.

The two met for the first time in August 2017. He had presented himself as an understanding listener, someone who not only shared her fears but also took them seriously. What she didn't know was that he had already rented a new apartment near Sobudaimae Station, specifically chosen for its seclusion and poor surveillance.

Shiraishi persuaded Mizuki to lend him a deposit for the apartment, and just a few days later, he invited her over. In the apartment, he gave her sleeping pills, waited until she fell asleep, and strangled her with a rope he had prepared. He then repeatedly assaulted her corpse; a cruel combination of sexual violence and total control. In the days that followed, he dismembered her body in the bathtub and stored the remains in coolers.

A few weeks later, on August 28, 2017, he lured his second victim to the same apartment: 15-year-old student Hongi Ishihara. She, too, was mentally unstable and had searched the internet for someone with whom she could talk openly about suicide. Shiraishi used the same tactics of understanding, closeness, and a feeling of connection. The killing was identical: sedation, strangulation, sexual violence, dismemberment.

Her parents soon reported her missing. The last location of her cell phone pointed to the same train station area as Mizuki's, but the police still had no connection.

The third victim, 20-year-old Takugo Nishinaki, knew Mizuki through social media. He, too, had struggled with suicidal thoughts and had fallen into a deep crisis after a failed relationship. He met with Shiraishi, initially to die, but then he changed his mind. He wrote to Shiraishi that he wanted to live.

That made him dangerous.

Shiraishi couldn't risk being discovered. He invited Takugo to his place again, drugged him, and killed him like the others. After the third murder, he stepped up his precautions against the smell of decay, buying cat litter, testing ventilation systems, and starting to dispose of body parts at night.

But the apartment had already become a morgue, and Shiraishi was a man with no way back.

After the third murder, Takahiro Shiraishi did not retreat. On the contrary, he seemed almost routine, as if a perfidious rhythm had settled in him. His apartment, which resembled a crime scene more than a home, became a trap for further victims.

His next target was Hinako Saraki, a 19-year-old student. She suffered from mental health issues, mainly caused by her mother's constant pressure to perform. She sought understanding on social media and came across Shiraishi. He played his role perfectly, understanding, calm, and trustworthy. On September 15, 2017, while his girlfriend at the time was away from home, he lured Hinako into the apartment, where the same gruesome scenario was repeated: drugging, strangulation, abuse, dismemberment.

Shortly thereafter, Hitomi Fujima came into Shiraishi's focus. The 26-year-old woman was already divorced, had to care for a disabled child on her own, and was facing another separation. In her desperation, she had spoken openly about her problems on the internet. Shiraishi saw this not as a story of suffering, but as an easy target.

When she met him, she was exhausted, mentally broken, but an unexpected call from her ex-husband, who suggested a meeting, threatened to thwart Shiraishi's plan. Before she could say goodbye, he silenced her, brutally and quickly. To reduce the stench of decay, he built a simple but effective ventilation system in his apartment.

He seemed unstoppable. Driven by a dark obsession, he exploited the invisibility of his victims, people whose disappearance raised few questions. Many of them were mentally unstable, lived on the margins of society, and had no strong family support. Shiraishi knew this, and he exploited it coldly, calculatingly, and methodically.

With five victims now in his apartment, not only did the smell grow, but so did the risk of being discovered. Instead of pausing, he stepped up his preparations. New coolers, more cat litter, better sealing, and new profiles on social networks, which he used to contact more potential victims.

He was convinced that if he controlled who entered the apartment, he was invulnerable.

But death had left its mark, and outside, beyond his locked door, people began to wonder where their loved ones had disappeared to.

Takahiro Shiraishi's series of murders had long since exceeded the limits of the imaginable, but the man who had now killed and dismembered five people felt no remorse. On the contrary, with each subsequent crime, he seemed to become more confident, more untouchable. The apartment, once inconspicuous, was now a silent witness to unprecedented horror.

In the fall of 2017, Shiraishi turned to the internet again. There, he specifically searched for people who spoke publicly about suicidal thoughts. He knew that those who seek death ask no questions. Those who are desperate are easier to control.

One of his next victims was a 25-year-old man who had fallen into deep depression due to family conflicts and financial problems. He had searched a platform for someone who would accompany him in his suicide. Shiraishi responded promptly with false compassion and insincere sympathy. In reality, he wanted only one thing: control. And another victim.

As with the others, he had prepared everything. The man was drugged, murdered, dismembered, and finally stowed away in one of the prepared boxes.

Two young women followed, both in their early twenties, both with mental health issues, both single. Shiraishi had approached them independently, read their stories, mirrored their fears, and convinced them to trust him. What they didn't know was that they were entering the apartment of a man who had long since lost all hope and knew only violence.

One came late in the evening, the other the following morning. Both died within 24 hours, and both were disposed of by Shiraishi with the same coldness as the previous victims.

The ninth and last person on his list was a 17-year-old schoolgirl. She had written about bullying and isolation on social media. Shiraishi contacted her via a newly created profile. His words sounded reassuring. He promised her a place of understanding, a safe space, but it was a lie.

When the girl entered his apartment, he had already prepared everything. She became the last person whose remains ended up in one of his boxes. The ninth box was full. A tenth was already waiting, but it remained empty.

Because even before Shiraishi could find his next victim, something had changed. The police were on his trail. Too many missing persons cases, too many last signs of life in the same area, and finally, a clue that would change everything.

The police had gradually recognized a pattern. Nine young people had disappeared without a trace within a few months, and all of them had previously talked about suicide on social media. The same area kept cropping up in their last digital traces: the vicinity of Suba-Daima station in the city of Zama.

When a young woman finally agreed to meet an anonymous man on Twitter, his messages became increasingly creepy. Something about them seemed strange to her, and she decided to inform the police. In close consultation with the investigators, she did not cancel the meeting. Instead, an undercover team, including the brother of one of the missing victims, accompanied the operation.

On October 30, 2017, the surveillance unit spotted a slim man with long black hair. He appeared to be waiting for someone. The officers discreetly followed him to a two-story building less than 800 meters from the train station. When the man entered the house, the investigators did not hesitate any longer. They knocked on the door, and a disgusting smell hit them. The man opened the door calmly, without resistance.

Inside, the police discovered a scene that shocked even experienced officers. There were nine large boxes in the apartment, filled with body parts. In one corner was a freezer covered with cat litter. Inside were nine human heads and hundreds of bone fragments. The walls were bare. In the bathroom were the tools used to carry out the murders: ropes, saws, and handcuffs. The man showed no remorse. He replied calmly when asked, "I killed them all. It was easy."

The man's name was Takahiro Shiraishi. He was 27 years old and unemployed. He had been carrying out a bloodbath in his apartment for months without arousing the suspicion of his neighbors or the authorities. There had been a foul smell, yes, but it had been attributed to the sewer system.

On November 9, the police identified all nine victims with the help of DNA tests. They were young people between the ages of 15 and 26. Almost all of them had suffered from depression or other mental illnesses. All of them had turned to the internet in desperation and found their killer there.

The trial began in the fall of 2020. Shiraishi made a full confession. He had no regrets, except that he had been caught. His defense attorney tried to claim mental illness, but the court saw no mitigating circumstances. On December 15, 2020, Takahiro Shiraishi was sentenced to death.

He did not appeal. Three days after the verdict, he stated that he no longer wanted to be a burden to anyone.

Watch the video

A profiler's opinion on this case

CASE 16

16. DECEMBER

On the morning of December 16, 1977, a gray Ford had been parked in the parking lot of the Quality Inn hotel in Hasbrouck Heights, New Jersey, for hours. An employee conducting a routine check noticed the vehicle, and when he looked inside, he discovered the lifeless body of a young woman in the back seat, who was naked, bound, and mutilated.

The police were alerted immediately, and the sight that met the investigators was gruesome: the woman, later identified as Maryann Carr, 26, had deep cuts on her chest and legs. Her wrists and ankles were covered with welts from being tied up. Her mouth was covered with duct tape, and there were bite marks on several parts of her body.

The last trace of her led to a parking lot in Little Ferry, where she had been seen the night before. She lived there, in the same apartment complex where a certain Richard Cottingham had once lived with his family.

At that point, Cottingham was a blank slate for investigators. No one suspected that the murder of Maryann Carr was not an isolated incident, but one in a whole series of violent crimes.

The Carr case ended up on the growing list of brutal, unsolved murders of women in the New York metropolitan area. The victims often came from marginalized groups, like women who worked in clubs, escorts, and runaways. They were women whose disappearances were hardly reported, and who were often alone.

Cottingham knew these weaknesses. He was not an impulsive perpetrator, but a hunter. His methods varied from case to case, sometimes drugs, sometimes bondage, sometimes fire. But the goal was always the same: total control.

No one suspected him of these crimes. He was 31 years old, married, had three children, and worked in an open-plan office at a health insurance company. His appearance? Inconspicuous. His environment? Average. His facade? Perfect.

But on the night of December 15-16, that facade faltered for a moment, and that was only the beginning.

The man who took Maryann Carr's life on December 16, 1977, was outwardly the exact opposite of a serial killer. Richard Francis Cottingham, born on November 25, 1946, in the Bronx, New York, grew up in a seemingly stable family. His father was an insurance clerk, his mother a housewife. As the eldest of three children, Richard was taught discipline from an early age; order, a sense of duty, and good grades. Nothing in his childhood indicated what was to come decades later.

However, Richard was a quiet, withdrawn boy. Early on, he developed a fascination with power and control, which initially manifested itself harmlessly in stories, comics, and later in erotic magazines. As he entered adolescence, he became increasingly interested in sadistic content. He didn't talk to anyone about it, and that's exactly what made him dangerous.

After graduating from high school in 1964, Cottingham joined the same insurance company where his father worked. He soon moved to the Blue Cross and Blue Shield Association, where he was considered a hard-working clerk in the years that followed. He was punctual, friendly, and reliable. In May 1970, he married Jeanette Winsky, and the couple had three children. The family moved to New Jersey. House, car, career; on paper, he was the kind of man many would wish for.

But while he filled out forms during the day and played with his children in the evening, another urge grew within him. A hunger for control, for submission. For violence.

The first known murder took place in 1967. Nancy Foggy, 29, married and mother of two, disappeared on her way to church. Hours later, she was found naked, bound, and dead in her car, with traces of sexual violence and strangulation marks, but no usable clues as to the perpetrator. The case was never solved. Years later, it turned out that Cottingham had known her personally. He knew exactly when and where she was going.

Two years later, in 1969, Cottingham was arrested for the first time for drunk driving. The sentence: ten days in jail and a $50 fine. No one raised the alarm. No one connected him to previous incidents.

In 1972, he came to attention again: he was caught shoplifting in a department store and reported for a violent assault on a woman, but there were no witnesses, no evidence. The charges were dropped.

His wife had no idea, and if she sensed something, she didn't say anything. Cottingham spent more and more time "at work," working overtime, often going to bed late, or staying out late. The reality was different: he roamed the streets of Manhattan, visited bars, and looked for women whom no one missed.

What made him so dangerous was his ability to adapt. He could disguise himself, appear charming, and seem harmless, but as soon as the door of a hotel room closed behind him, the mask disappeared, and the monster emerged.

In May 1980, just under two and a half years after the murder of Maryann Carr, 18-year-old Leslie Ann O'Dell came to New York. She had run away from home, from the confines, from her problems. Like many young women who hoped to build a better life in this city, she ended up on the streets, without money, without a plan. She quickly fell prey to pimps who were specifically looking for "fresh meat." Leslie agreed to sleep with strange men for money. She had no choice.

On May 22, just four days after her arrival, Leslie was standing on Lexington Avenue when a man approached her. Well-groomed, friendly, with a calm voice. He seemed educated, honest, and almost empathetic. Leslie was often cautious and suspicious, but he seemed different. She agreed to have sex with him for $180. They checked into the Quality Inn hotel and went to her room.

Around 5:00 a.m., he suggested giving her a massage. Leslie lay down on her stomach, and the moment she relaxed, the friendly man turned into a brutal attacker.

He took a knife out of a briefcase, pressed it to her throat, handcuffed her, and began to systematically torture her. He bit her breast, made small cuts on her back with the knife, and beat her with a leather belt. "You're a parasite," he said. "And you're going to pay for what you do."

Leslie screamed, and that's what saved her life. Just 18 days earlier, a woman had been murdered in that hotel, so the staff were on high alert. When there was a knock at the door, the perpetrator forced Leslie to open it at gunpoint and threatened to shoot her if she made a sound or tried to escape. She knew that any wrong move could be her last, but she managed to signal to the employee with a barely perceptible glance that she was in danger. The employee reacted immediately and alerted the police.

When the officers stormed the room, the perpetrator was no longer there, but he didn't get far. Just a few minutes later, he was arrested in the hallway with a briefcase containing handcuffs, a leather gag, two collars, a knife, a pistol, and several sedatives.

His name: Richard Cottingham.

At first, he claimed that Leslie had been with him voluntarily. She was a prostitute, he said, and it had been "consensual," but Leslie disagreed. In her statement, she described every minute of the horror with shocking detail, and mentioned a sentence that caught the investigators' attention: he had forced her to take pills "like the others."

"The others." With this one expression, she opened the door to a past full of violence and death, and she gave the investigators the crucial clue they needed to link Cottingham to a whole series of unsolved murders.

After Richard Cottingham's arrest and Leslie O'Dell's testimony, the investigators began a race against time. They now knew that this man was not a random perpetrator. He was prepared, structured, and probably a repeat offender.

The reference to "the others" led investigators to search specifically for similar cases, and they found what they were looking for, faster than they thought.

Just two weeks before the attack on Leslie, on May 5, 1980, the body of a young woman had been discovered in the same Quality Inn in South Hackensack. She was handcuffed, her mouth taped shut, and her body covered with bite marks and bruises. The woman's name was Valerie Ann Street, 19 years old, originally from Florida, who had recently moved to New York to work as an escort. The perpetrator had introduced himself as "John." After that, he disappeared without a trace.

This time, though, he had made a mistake. During the forensic examination of Valerie's body, the handcuffs were carefully examined, and a partial thumbprint was found on one of the shackles. At the time, investigators had no reference sample, but now, with Cottingham in custody, the comparison yielded a clear match.

The man who had killed Valerie was the same man who tortured Leslie. The connection was there.

The investigators now picked apart Cottingham's past. They searched for hotels where he had stayed. Names under which he had booked rooms. Phone numbers, credit cards, working hours. A pattern emerged, one that had been so well hidden that it could only be seen as obvious from today's perspective.

He had regularly booked hotel rooms under false names such as "Carl Wilson" or "Jim Schaefer." Always near bus stations or red-light districts, always alone, and always for just one night.

His bookings were compared with unsolved deaths. One case from December 1979 was particularly striking. At that time, two charred, decapitated female corpses had been found at the Travel Inn in New York. In room 417, which had been booked a few days earlier under the name Carl Wilson.

The victims had no fingerprints left. Their faces had been made unrecognizable. Their bodies had been tied up, their clothes neatly folded in the bathroom. The perpetrator had brutally tortured them, severed their heads and hands, and set the room on fire. Nothing was more important to him than ensuring they could not be identified.

Now that Cottingham's modus operandi was known, it became clear that this was also his work.

He had proceeded methodically. He was thoughtful, disciplined, and at the same time cruel to the point of perversion. With each new piece of evidence, each secure lead, it became clear to investigators that Richard Cottingham was not just a violent criminal. He was a strategic serial killer who had been killing women undetected for years and covering his tracks like a pro.

The prosecution obtained a search warrant for Cottingham's house in Lodi, New Jersey, where he had lived with his family. What the investigators found there was definitive proof that these were not just isolated cases.

In the basement of the house, they came across a hidden chamber behind a seemingly solid shelf. Inside this chamber was a kind of trophy collection, neatly stowed away, as if in an archive.

It contained women's underwear, makeup bags, hair accessories, notebooks, photos, jewelry, and a pair of high heels that could later be traced to one of the unknown victims.

To an outsider, it was a chaotic collection of random items. To Cottingham, it was an altar, a collection of moments of power, memories of submission, control, dominance. Each piece carried a story, a cry that no one heard anymore.

At the same time, investigators found a list of names, phone numbers, and room numbers in an old briefcase, seemingly harmless, but when checked against police records, several of the women listed appeared in missing persons reports. Some of them had been found dead, some were never identified, and some were never searched for.

Cottingham himself denied everything. He explained that the items belonged to former partners, that they were "old memories" that he had "kept out of courtesy." The fingerprints on the handcuffs? A mistake. Leslie's statements? Lies. The bite marks? Coincidence. The basement room? A "private storage room."

His calmness was almost frightening. He spoke clearly, matter-of-factly, without remorse. He repeatedly emphasized: "I am not a murderer. I am a victim."

However, the burden of proof grew. The prosecution soon officially charged him with multiple murders. Initially, he was charged with two murders: Valerie Ann Street, one of the decapitated women from the Travel Inn, and Maryann Carr, whose body had been found on December 16, 1977.

In addition, there were attempted murders and rapes, including in the cases of Leslie O'Dell and Pamela Weisenfeld.

When Cottingham's ex-wife learned of the allegations, she collapsed. She had suspected that her husband had "a dark side," but not to this extent. He often worked overtime and didn't come home for days, so she thought he was having an affair, not committing murders.

The police now spoke publicly of a serial killer, possibly with more than a dozen victims, and at the center of the investigation was a man whom no one had even suspected for years.

The trial of Richard Cottingham began in 1982. The charges were extensive: murder, attempted murder, rape, kidnapping, and assault. There were six specific crimes, but investigators had long suspected that the actual number was much higher.

Cottingham appeared calm, composed, and almost arrogant in the courtroom. He was convinced that nothing could be proven against him, but on the very first day of the trial, it became clear that the evidence was overwhelming.

– Fingerprints on the handcuffs

– Matching DNA traces

– Witness statements from surviving women

– Trophies from his secret basement

– Handwritten notes that matched hotel bookings

But what made the trial so special was not only the evidence, but Cottingham's own statements.

In a surprising turn of events, he confessed in court that he had been fascinated by the idea of total submission since his youth. As a teenager, he read pornographic magazines with sadistic content and was interested in stories about domination and bondage. "I wanted control," he said. "And I got it." He spoke about his actions not as crimes, but as personal achievements.

These statements shocked not only the audience in the courtroom but also experienced investigators. Cottingham showed no remorse, no compassion, no guilt. He was completely disconnected from human reality. A man who had learned to simulate emotions and, at the same time, to extinguish the lives of others without batting an eyelid.

After several weeks of trial, the court handed down its verdict: a total of more than 200 years in prison, with no prospect of early release, but the story did not end there.

In the decades that followed, while he was in prison, Cottingham repeatedly contacted journalists, authors, and investigators. He played with them as he had played with his victims. He claimed to be responsible for over 100 murders. "There are many you don't know about," he once told a reporter. And indeed, in the years that followed, he confessed to several other crimes that had remained unsolved until then.

Some of these statements led to new investigations. In several cases, archived evidence proved his guilt. This brought the number of his confirmed victims to at least 18.

Watch the video

A profiler's opinion on this case

CASE 17

17. DECEMBER

On December 17, 1977, a man named Joe Cleveland disappeared along with his girlfriend, Liddie Matthews Evans. The two were last seen alive when they visited Carl Millard Patton, a quiet, seemingly average family man from Georgia, USA. That evening, Patton killed the couple with a shotgun, hid the bodies in sleeping bags, and sank them in the Flint River. For over two decades, this crime remained unsolved.

It was not until 2003, when Patton was convicted using modern DNA technology, that investigators refocused their attention on the old cases. However, it was the confessions of his wife, Norma, that prompted investigators to re-examine the evidence. This started a chain of revelations that went far beyond the original murders. The re-examination of evidence and DNA profiles brought another crime to light: the death of his own daughter, Melissa Wolfenbarger.

In 1998, Melissa was a 21-year-old woman, married, and a mother of two, living in Atlanta. She had a difficult marriage with Christopher Wolfenbarger, who, according to her family, was violent. On November 26, 1998, Thanksgiving Day, Melissa spoke to her mother, Norma, on the phone for the last time. She talked about Christmas preparations and said she would come to visit soon, but she never came. Christmas passed without a word, which was unusual and worrying.

In January 1999, Norma and her husband drove to Melissa's apartment on Brooklyn Avenue. The rooms were empty, as if someone had moved out in a hurry. No note, no clue, no address left behind. Neighbors said the couple had disappeared between Christmas and New Year's. The police were not called in at first.

In April 1999, a black garbage bag was found in a wooded area near Atlanta. Inside was a human head. Two months later, in June, more body parts were found in the same area, also in bags. At first, it was believed to be an older male homeless person, so the remains were buried anonymously. There was no DNA match, and no one linked the discovery to Melissa.

It was only years later, after Patton's arrest, that an investigator remembered the old findings. By comparing them with Melissa's DNA, which was available through her children, the identification was made in 2003: they were her remains. Suddenly, the young mother's disappearance was no longer just a missing person case. It was murder—brutal, planned, and cold-blooded.

What had previously appeared to be a family tragedy now took on new contours. Who had killed Melissa? Why was her body dismembered, packed into trash bags, and hidden? And what role did her father, Carl Patton, play, who was charged with several other murders at the same time?

After Melissa's remains were identified in 2003, investigators were certain that this was a murder case and that the perpetrator must have come from her immediate circle. It was a murder with a personal connection, and suspicion immediately fell on two people: her father, Carl Patton, and her husband, Christopher Wolfenbarger.

Carl Patton was already known in the media as a serial killer at that time. His confession included several killings in the 1970s, including the murders of Joe Cleveland and Liddie Evans in December 1977, the crime that had started this whole chain of revelations. However, in Melissa's case, he denied any responsibility. He insisted he had nothing to do with his daughter's death, and indeed, there was no forensic evidence linking him to the location where the body was found.

Christopher Wolfenbarger, on the other hand, made himself look suspicious through his behavior. He had been known for domestic violence on several occasions in the past. Witnesses reported that Melissa had been oppressed in the relationship and that she was afraid of him. Her sister Tina later testified that Melissa had repeatedly confided in her that she wanted to leave, that she couldn't take it anymore, but she stayed because of the children and the hope that things would get better.

After Melissa's disappearance in the winter of 1998, Christopher showed no initiative whatsoever. He did not report her missing, did not ask anyone about her, and did not inform the authorities. Even after the body was identified in 2003, he remained passive, evaded questions, and refused to cooperate with the police. It seemed as if he wanted to close the chapter on Melissa as quickly as possible.

Investigators tried to get him to talk, but he insisted on remaining silent. He was questioned several times but never formally charged. The final piece of evidence was missing; no confession, no direct evidence. Melissa was dead, her body destroyed, her last days shrouded in darkness, and without witnesses or forensic evidence, the case remained officially unsolved.

Norma, Melissa's mother, did not give up. She fought tirelessly for answers, gathering clues, talking to the media, and urging the police to re-examine the case. For her, it was clear: her daughter had been the victim of a crime, and she deserved justice. As more time passed, the harder it became to gain new insights. Many clues had faded, witnesses had forgotten important details, or no longer wanted to remember.

For Norma and Tina, Melissa's mother and sister, a new phase of grief began, one accompanied by anger, powerlessness, and a sense of injustice. They had waited over four years for a sign, for an explanation, for the truth. Now it was there, but it was incomplete. Melissa was dead, but the circumstances of her death remained unclear. There was no trial, no perpetrator, no official explanation. Just a few garbage bags in the woods and a silence louder than any confession.

Norma went public. She gave interviews, told Melissa's story, and demanded that the investigation be reopened. She talked about the violence in Melissa's marriage, about the constant tension, and about her daughter's fear. About Christopher's silence and his escape from responsibility, but the police remained cautious. Without new evidence, the investigators could do nothing. A vague suspicion was not enough for an indictment.

To make matters worse, Carl Patton began to withdraw again. After his comprehensive confession to the crimes of the 1970s, he refused to cooperate any further. He responded evasively to questions about Melissa. He repeated that he had nothing to do with it, and he left open the question of whether he knew more than he was saying. For many investigators, this was a tactic; he controlled the information he disclosed. He gave them only as much as he wanted to, and as far as Melissa was concerned, he apparently wanted to remain silent.

In 2004, the family had renewed hope: a new DNA analysis, a forgotten clue, a witness from back then, anything that might help, but once again, everything came to nothing. The files were closed, and the case was considered a "cold case." Melissa had been identified, but her killer remained at large.

For Norma and Tina, the search for answers became their life's work. They founded an initiative for missing women, held vigils, and spoke at events. They didn't want Melissa to be forgotten. They wanted someone to take responsibility, and they wanted a line in the police report that said, "Case closed. Perpetrator identified."

But that line was never written.

The years passed, but the questions remained. Their daughter Tina had grown up, but she too carried the burden of the past. They both talked about Melissa regularly. It wasn't a past that could simply be left behind; it was an open wound. Every news report about a missing person, every new cold case project brought hope. Hope that there would be movement in Melissa's case again.

In 2010, Norma contacted the authorities again. She handed over everything she had collected: letters, notes, old photos, and names of people who had known Melissa, but much of it was no longer verifiable. The only thing that remained was the memory, and the conviction that someone knew what had happened.

In Atlanta, the investigating authorities had become more professional. There were new techniques and new units for unsolved cases, but Melissa's case remained difficult. The body parts that had been found had been misidentified for years. The failure to compare DNA earlier had allowed the trail to go cold. By the time her identity had finally been established, it was too late for many lines of investigation. The crime scene had never been found, and there were no witness statements for the crucial period of time. Not a single name came up in connection with the trash bags.

Meanwhile, Christopher Wolfenbarger continued to live in Georgia. He had custody of their two children, a circumstance that was almost unbearable for Norma.

The idea that her grandchildren were growing up with the man she believed responsible for her daughter's death was unbearable, but here, too, her hands were tied. The authorities saw no immediate reason to revoke custody. Wolfenbarger himself never commented publicly on the case. He gave no interviews, no explanations, no statements.

Tina recalled meeting him once at an event. It was not an official appointment, but rather a coincidence. She later said that his gaze was empty, no regret, no remorse, just distance. She had tried to confront him, but he had left without saying a word. For her, this encounter was symbolic: the man she believed to be guilty simply carried on with his life as if nothing had happened.

Norma, on the other hand, channeled her pain into activism. Her daughter was dead, but through her efforts, she hoped to at least prevent other mothers from suffering a similar fate.

Yet a slight doubt remained. What if they were wrong? What if it wasn't Wolfenbarger who was responsible, but someone else? Perhaps even Carl Patton himself, despite his denials? Or a complete stranger? The uncertainty gnawed at them, not knowing the who, when, where, why, and how Melissa died, was sometimes worse than the grief itself.

In 2013, exactly 15 years after Melissa's disappearance, a local newspaper in Georgia published a retrospective on unsolved criminal cases. One of the sections was dedicated to Melissa. It stated matter-of-factly: "Investigation closed. No new leads. Perpetrator unknown." For Norma, it was like a slap in the face. All her efforts, her constant pushing, the media coverage, and yet in the end, all that remained was a single sentence in a year-in-review.

She pasted the clipping into her notebook and wrote underneath it in red pen: "But I know who did it." It was her silent protest against a system that wanted to forget her and her daughter. She repeatedly contacted journalists, investigators, and organizations, but the longer the case was closed, the less interest there was; one cold case among thousands.

In the meantime, Christopher Wolfenbarger had rebuilt his life. He worked, raised his children, remarried. He was considered unremarkable in the neighborhood. No one talked about Melissa anymore. The children, now teenagers, knew little about what had happened to their mother. Norma was rarely allowed to see them, and when she did, it was under supervision. The relationship was strained, and every visit reminded her of what she had lost and who she believed was to blame.

The investigation file had become a silent archive document. The few photos of Melissa, the forensic reports, the DNA results, everything was stored in a folder labeled "Wolfenbarger, Melissa—1998–2003." In between: handwritten notes, loose sheets of paper with questions that were never answered.

She contacted the police one last time in 2018. She had written a five-page letter summarizing the most important points: Melissa's fear, her planned move, Christopher's behavior after the disappearance, and his silence. She did not ask for charges to be brought; she knew how difficult that was, but she asked for the case to be officially reopened. It was read, archived, and not pursued further.

Carl Patton was in prison, serving a life sentence. He never spoke to Melissa again. His only statement remained: "I didn't do it." No remorse, no denial, no explanation. Some believed him; others thought it was a protective claim, but without evidence, it all remained speculation.

For Norma, that didn't change anything. For her, it was clear: Carl hadn't killed Melissa. He had been capable of many things, but not that. Not his own daughter. She firmly believed that it had been Wolfenbarger. Maybe it wasn't planned. Maybe it was in a moment of anger. Maybe it was an argument that escalated, but she believed it was him.

In 2021, Norma took part in a local radio project called "Voices of the Forgotten." On the show, she talked about her daughter, about Thanksgiving 1998, about the phone call that never came, about the trash bags in the woods, and about the police who never did enough. At the end, she said, "I don't know if I'll live to see it, but I hope that one day someone will say, 'It wasn't for nothing.'"

The program was broadcast in Georgia, though not many people heard it, but for Norma, it was important. It was her last public statement—a legacy. She wanted the world to know who Melissa was: not an anonymous dead person, but a daughter, mother, sister, wife who deserved better than the end she had met.

Wolfenbarger did not respond to the broadcast. His children never commented either. For them, the chapter had long been closed, if it had ever really been open.

In an interview with a distant relative, they said, "They don't talk about it. It's as if it never happened." Perhaps it was self-protection. Perhaps repression. Perhaps also a silent admission.

Carl Patton died in prison in 2022. Heart attack. No last words, no letter, no new confessions. With him, much information about his past deeds also disappeared. Some investigators had hoped he would say something shortly before his death, a final confession, a name, a detail, but nothing came. He remained silent about Melissa until the end.

After his death, the folder with Melissa's name was opened once again. Not out of police interest, but because Norma organized a memorial service. She invited friends, relatives, and former neighbors. They talked about Melissa, told anecdotes, and showed photos. It was a quiet, dignified farewell more than 20 years after her death. "Finally, a place to mourn," Tina said quietly.

Today, there is no longer any mention of Melissa Wolfenbarger in official records. The case remains unsolved. No perpetrator has ever been charged. The garbage bags in the forest have long since been disposed of, the evidence lost, and the traces faded.

Sometimes, Norma said in one of her last interviews, she still goes to the woods where Melissa was found. She imagines how she might have lain there. Not because she wants to torment herself, but because she wants to feel that Melissa is not forgotten. That someone still says her name. That she existed.

Watch the video

A profiler's opinion on this case

CASE 18

18. DECEMBER

On December 18, 1988, 51-year-old Kent Alan Lauten was found dead in Tucson, Arizona, stabbed to death and buried in a shallow grave near a homeless camp. His body was discovered two days later. The perpetrator, a certain Tommy Lynn Sells, later testified that he had killed Lauten because he had refused to pay for drugs, and no one suspected that this was already Sells's eighth victim. It was not until many years later, after another murder committed on December 31, 1999, that the true extent of his crimes came to light.

On that New Year's Eve, the horror took on a new form in the neighboring state of Texas. Ten-year-old Krystal Surles lived with her family in the small town of Del Rio. Her parents were planning to move from Texas to Kansas, and since the old house was already almost empty, Krystal and her younger sister, Markie, were allowed to spend New Year's Eve at their new friend Kaylene Harris's house. The girls were full of anticipation—a new year, a new home, and new friendships.

Kaylene Harris lived with her mother and siblings in a simple house on the outskirts of town. On New Year's Eve, the children watched movies together, ate popcorn, and made themselves comfortable. No one suspected that the house would soon become the scene of a crime that would cause nationwide horror.

Kaylene and Krystal slept together in one room, and in the early hours of January 1, 2000, Krystal was awakened by a scream. Still half asleep, she noticed that the light was on and that a strange man was standing at the bottom of her loft bed. It was Tommy Lynn Sells. He covered Kaylene's mouth and stabbed her in the neck with a knife. Krystal froze. The man hadn't noticed her, not yet.

As the perpetrator turned to leave, he saw Krystal. Without hesitation, he grabbed the girl, pulled her out of bed, and stabbed her in the neck as well. Then he turned off the light, left the room, and closed the door behind him.

Despite her serious injury, Krystal remained alive. With her last ounce of strength, she crawled to Kaylene, but her friend was already dead. The house was silent. Not a sound, no sign of movement. Krystal suspected the worst: that the perpetrator had murdered everyone in the house.

Injured, bleeding, and terrified, Krystal finally pulled herself together. She crept through the house looking for her little sister, Markie, but she couldn't speak and therefore couldn't warn her. The house was silent, and her fear grew. Krystal firmly believed that the killer might still be somewhere in the house.

Despite her serious injuries, she decided to get help. In her nightgown and with a gaping wound on her neck, she stumbled out into the cold night. It was January 1, the sky was dark, and the air was icy, but Krystal didn't let that stop her. In the distance, she spotted a light from a neighbor's house about a kilometer away. Barefoot and covered in blood, she set off.

When she finally reached the front door, she knocked weakly. The man in the house hesitated at first, but when he saw the injured ten-year-old, he opened the door immediately. She couldn't speak, so he handed her a pen and a piece of paper. With a trembling hand, she wrote: "Hurry with the ambulance" and "Will I survive?" The man tried to calm her down, dialed the emergency number, and did his best to stabilize the injured girl until the paramedics arrived.

A short time later, an ambulance arrived and took Krystal to a nearby hospital. The doctors fought for her life. The neck wound was deep, and she had lost a lot of blood. No one knew yet whether she would survive. Meanwhile, the police arrived at the Harris family home. Kaylene was dead, and her mother and the other children had been unaware of what had happened. Markie was also unharmed, having slept deeply and only opening her eyes when the police were already in the house.

The investigators, now faced with a brutal murder and attempted homicide, initially focused on the surviving witness: Krystal. After undergoing emergency surgery and being stabilized, she was transferred to a larger hospital in San Antonio. There, doctors carefully monitored her condition while her mother remained by her side.

Despite her serious injuries, Krystal was conscious and soon able to speak again. Her first question was about her friend Kaylene. Her mother hesitated at first to tell her the truth, but Krystal insisted. When she learned of her friend's death, she was devastated, but also determined. She wanted the killer caught.

The police called in a sketch artist. Krystal described the perpetrator in detail: long, dark hair, an unkempt beard, angry eyes. When the artist had finished the sketch, Krystal recognized him immediately: "He looks exactly like him." The officers began searching databases and comparing photos of convicted criminals. Finally, they showed Krystal a selection, and she didn't hesitate: she pointed silently at a photo.

The man in the picture was Tommy Lynn Sells. He was 35 years old, lived in Del Rio, very close by, and had an extensive criminal history. The police immediately made their way to his home. It was a mobile home. They knocked, but no one answered. The door was slightly ajar, so they entered and found Tommy Sells inside.

He looked at them calmly and said, "I'm glad I finally got caught. I'm tired of doing this." Without asking what he was being arrested for, he allowed himself to be handcuffed. That same day, he confessed to the crime in great detail.

Tommy Lynn Sells described to investigators in detail what had happened on the night of the crime. He had entered the Harris family's home through an open window. According to his statement, he had moved quietly through the house, seeing all the sleeping residents. His target was Kaylene; he knew her vaguely and had already chosen her. He approached her, cut her underwear with a knife, and tried to sexually abuse her, but the girl broke free and started screaming.

Sells reacted immediately. He covered her mouth, grabbed his knife, and stabbed her several times in the neck. He then wanted to leave the house, but then he noticed Krystal, who was lying stiff and distraught in the upper bed. She had seen everything, so Sells decided to silence her too. He pulled her toward him, stabbed her in the neck, turned off the light, and left the house. He was convinced that both girls were dead.

The police had him accompany them to the scene of the crime. Without hesitation, Sells reconstructed the crime, showing how he had moved, how he had opened the window, and wielded the knife, smiling as he did so. It quickly became clear to the investigators that this man felt no remorse. On the contrary, he seemed proud of what he had done.

The longer they talked to him, the clearer it became that this was not his first murder. Although Sells had mainly been known in the past for theft, assault, and drunk driving, he had also raped a woman once and been sentenced to four years in prison for it. The investigators now began to suspect that there was much more to his criminal history.

Sells began to talk, more than the investigators had expected. On the way back from the Harris family home, he suddenly said, "I guess you want to know about the others." And then he opened up. Over the course of several weeks, he talked about his childhood, abuse, violence, and the beginning of his criminal career. His mother was overwhelmed with raising him, his twin sister died young, and Sells began drinking at the age of seven.

At ten, he was raped himself. Shortly thereafter, he tried to approach his own mother, naked, in the middle of the night. The family did not respond with help, but with flight: they moved away and left Sells behind. From then on, he lived on the streets, got drunk regularly, and committed burglaries and thefts. At fifteen, he claimed, he committed his first murder, a man shot in his own home; the case remained unsolved.

Since then, he said, he had traveled across the US and committed numerous murders. In conversations with the police, he confessed to over a hundred crimes. Investigators began to verify his statements and quickly realized that much of it was exaggerated, some of it fabricated, but in at least 17 cases, his statements matched unsolved crimes exactly. In these cases, they considered him guilty beyond a doubt, even though there was often no physical evidence left.

Sells enjoyed the attention. He described the crimes with frightening composure, almost as if he were telling stories from an adventure novel. It was clear that fame and impact were more important to him than the truth. If a crime brought him attention, he was willing to take credit for it, even if he hadn't committed it.

In 2000, Sells confessed to the murder of Kaylene Harris and the attack on Krystal, as well as 22 other killings, including those of three children. However, because the police found no conclusive evidence, he was ultimately charged with only two counts: the murder of Kaylene and the attempted murder of Krystal. The trial began six months after his arrest, and the prosecution sought the death penalty. Krystal, now almost fully recovered physically, was determined to testify against him. She described the night in detail, looking him straight in the eye. Sells lowered his gaze. The defense presented no arguments in favor of the perpetrator. The verdict was death, and Sells was transferred to death row.

Fourteen years later, in 2014, the sentence was carried out. In addition to Kaylene's relatives, the families of other alleged victims were present at the execution, as well as Krystal. When asked for his last words, Sells replied, "None." He just looked at a few acquaintances and smiled. Krystal, however, had never really found peace since then. She slept poorly, planned escape routes at night, and imagined what she would do if he came back. Her relationship with her sisters improved, as they now understood why Krystal had been so assertive in the past; out of concern, not arrogance.

Even after Tommy Sells' death, the story did not end. In 2015, a woman who had seen a documentary about him came forward. Her mother had been murdered in 1982, and the caller herself and her sister had been injured. Another man, Rodney Lincoln, had been convicted, but the woman now recognized Sells as the real perpetrator. Lincoln was released after 36 years in prison, at the age of 77.

A year later, in 2016, Krystal was threatened online. A man sent her photos of crime scenes, accused her of not saving Kaylene, threatened to kill her, and even sent her her own address. Fortunately, the police were able to find him quickly. Krystal has given several interviews since then. She said she was just glad to be alive. She no longer thinks about Sells. His true number of victims will probably never be known, but at least he is dead and can no longer harm anyone.

Sells had no home, no permanent address. He hitchhiked across the country, striking everywhere, silently and without a trace. The police eventually called him "The Coast to Coast Killer." His tracks were scattered across the country, but one victim survived, and she spoke out. And through her voice, his silence ended, and so did his life.

Watch the video

A profiler's opinion on this case

CASE 19

19. DECEMBER

On the morning of December 19, 2014, Lewis Guardia, a 20-year-old young man, took the bus to his mother's house at 34 Murray Street in the suburb of Manoora, Cairns, Australia. When he arrived, he found his mother, Raina Thaiday, barefoot on the porch. Her clothes were dirty, her gaze empty. She had inflicted 35 stab wounds on herself in her chest, neck, and arms. She was still alive. Without saying a word, she beckoned him to come closer with her finger, but Lewis felt uneasy; something was wrong.

He tried to find out from his mother what had happened, but the only thing she said was, "I killed them." No crying. No explanations. Just that one sentence. Lewis cautiously entered the house. There was an unnatural silence, and then he saw it. A scene that would be burned into his memory forever.

Inside the house lay eight lifeless bodies: four boys and four girls; his seven siblings and his cousin.

The youngest of the victims was one and a half years old, the oldest fourteen. Some were lying on mattresses, others on the floor. Their bodies looked peaceful. Almost as if they were sleeping, but there was no doubt, they were dead. Lewis left the house, took a few steps, then returned. He didn't know what to do.

Finally, at 11:20 a.m., he called the police. They found Thaiday with her injuries, but she had survived.

The crime shocked not only Cairns but the entire country. Eight children murdered in a suburb, in a simple wooden house, amid the contemplative pre-Christmas season. A family wiped out. A mother, the alleged perpetrator.

What had happened that night? How could a woman who was considered loving, religious, and hospitable be capable of such an act? The police were baffled. Raina Thaiday was taken to the hospital with serious injuries. She spoke incoherently, her statements seeming to come from another world.

The investigation began immediately. It was not just a murder case; it was a family massacre. Neighbors reported strange occurrences in the weeks leading up to the incident. Thaiday had thrown furniture out of the house, scrubbed walls, and sung religious songs. She had spoken of the end being near, and she had urged her children to cleanse themselves, physically and spiritually.

In retrospect, all of this seemed like omens, but no one had any idea what was to come.

In retrospect, the hours before the crime seemed like the slow collapse of an already troubled psyche. On the evening of December 18, 2014, two girls, Thaiday's daughter and her goddaughter, asked permission to leave the house to go shopping. Thaiday allowed them to go on the condition that they return by 10 p.m., but the clock ticked on, and no one came back. Around midnight, Thaiday began pacing up and down the street, calling out her children's names, praying the Lord's Prayer aloud, and cursing supposed attackers who were targeting her family. She screamed: "I am the chosen one! I have the power to destroy people!" Neighbors heard her threaten to stab anyone who would harm her children.

Around 1:30 a.m., her daughter returned, alone. The nervousness on Thaiday's face did not subside. Her goddaughter had not accompanied her daughter back home but had made her own way home. What happened inside the house after that can only be reconstructed based on forensic findings and Thaiday's later statements.

The next morning, before Lewis Guardia entered the house, Thaiday had already attempted to kill herself. She stabbed herself 35 times with a knife, mainly in the chest and neck area. She survived thanks to medical coincidence and quick intervention. She was immediately taken to Cairns Base Hospital and operated on.

On December 21, the police officially charged Raina Thaiday with eight counts of murder. While still in the hospital, she spoke to the authorities, not in a legal sense, but in a state of religious ecstasy. She said she knew that people would now hate her, but she was convinced that she had done the right thing. Her children were "pure," and she had protected them from evil, as God had commanded her to do so.

The house on Murray Street became a symbol of a family tragedy. Media representatives from all over Australia gathered there. The neighborhood placed candles, flowers, stuffed animals, and handwritten cards in front of the gate. A tree in front of the house was covered with a white curtain. It served as a silent altar.

On December 22, the victims' relatives gathered for an impromptu ceremony at this very tree. Toys, roses, prayers, anything that could ease the pain a little. The father of four of the children who were killed, Gayon Wiliye, stood there crying with a lovingly packed parcel full of memories for his children. "My children, my children," he sobbed repeatedly as he clutched the small parcel tightly to his chest. It was a silent, deeply moving moment, a farewell that no parent should ever have to experience.

The days following the crime were marked by collective grief and a search for answers. In a press conference, community representative Jodie Baczky asked for consideration for the grieving family. At the same time, public interest in the case grew. How could a mother be capable of such an act? Had there been warning signs? Could something have been done to prevent it?

The investigation soon revealed that Raina Thaiday had been suffering from mental health problems for years. She had already been in crisis in 2007, shaving her head and threatening one of her children. Two years later, she attempted to take her own life. Despite this, she had never received comprehensive psychiatric treatment, only occasional consultations with an indigenous health service. In the weeks before the crime, her behavior had changed dramatically: she had become fanatically religious, threw furniture out of the house, cleaned obsessively, slept outside with the children, and spoke of purification and divine mission; but no one recognized the danger.

On January 10, 2015, a memorial service was held at the Cairns Convention Centre. Over 4,000 people attended, many of them members of the Torres Strait community where Thaiday came from. The ceremony was entitled "Our Children" and was held in the language of the indigenous population. Australian Prime Minister Tony Abbott was also present. In his speech, he spoke of solidarity, of protecting the most vulnerable, and of the need to take mental illness seriously.

At the end of January, Raina Thaiday was transferred to the psychiatric hospital in Brisbane. The trial was to take place before the Mental Health Court, not before a normal criminal court. There, psychiatrists and judges jointly decided whether the defendant had been criminally responsible at the time of the offense. It was a rare occurrence as Australia has strict criteria for such proceedings.

The experts, including Dr. Angela Volta and Dr. Pamela Vandehef, came to a clear conclusion: Raina Thaiday suffered from paranoid schizophrenia. Her delusions had apocalyptic traits. She believed that the end of the world was imminent. Her children were in danger, and only death could save them. The act arose from this distorted reality, not from hatred or intent.

Dr. Vandehef emphasized that Thaiday posed no danger to the public as long as she was receiving treatment, but the treatment was slow to take effect. Even in the clinic, she continued to talk about voices, about God's commands, about the need to kill others. The risk of relapse was considered high. She should only be allowed to leave the clinic under strict supervision, and even then, only for a limited period of time.

On May 3, 2017, the Mental Health Court handed down its verdict: Raina Thaiday was not criminally responsible at the time of the crime. She had suffered from severe, untreated paranoid schizophrenia and was convinced that she was doing the right thing. Therefore, under Queensland law, she could not be held criminally responsible. The decision was legally clear and, at the same time, emotionally distressing. Many wondered how such a tragic failure of the system had been possible.

The signs had been there: previous incidents of violence, religious delusions, increasing isolation, dramatic mood swings, but no one had acted. There was no psychological care, no crisis intervention, no protection for the children. The family was left alone with their despair, and with an illness that spread inexorably.

After the verdict, Raina Thaiday was permanently committed to a forensic psychiatric facility. Although no prison sentence was imposed, a life of freedom was no longer an option. The doctors explained that Thaiday continued to show symptoms even during treatment. She spoke of divine destiny, expressed violent fantasies, and reacted unpredictably to medication. Release would only be possible under the strictest supervision, and was out of the question in the foreseeable future.

On December 1, 2018, an emotional ceremony took place in Cairns: the solemn unveiling of the gravestones of the eight children. The so-called "Tombstone Opening Ceremony" is a deeply rooted tradition of the Torres Strait community, marking the official end of the mourning period. On that day, more than 4,000 people gathered in front of the graves to lay flowers, pray, and commemorate the deceased together.

The gravestones had been covered with colorful cloths, which were ceremoniously removed during the ceremony. The names engraved were: Malili, Shantay, Torensa Guardia, Assari, Daniela, Rodney, Petronella, and Villia Thaiday. Those present held hands, sang songs, and wept quietly. It was a moment of dignity, farewell, and collective hope.

Joseph Elu, a respected spokesperson for the Torres Strait Authority, addressed the mourners in a moving speech, "These children were the light of our community. Their names will live on. Their memory is our responsibility." The father of four of the children, Gayon Wiliye, later told the press that he thinks about his children every day, and that to this day, there is no answer as to why.

The verdict was followed by years of silence. Raina Thaiday remained in a secure psychiatric facility, far from the public eye. Only two of her children, Lewis, who had entered the house in 2014 and found the bodies, and Norina, were still alive and kept in touch. In a 2016 interview, Lewis talked about how deeply the trauma had affected him. His siblings, his entire childhood, had been wiped out, and yet he visited his mother. He had a tattoo done on his forearm: eight birds in flight and the words "I will carry you with me until I see you again." A silent reminder that accompanied his grief.

In 2020, Australian media reported on the case again. It concerned an internal report that showed that many warning signs had been ignored in the run-up to the incident. The experts concluded that Thaiday had suffered from untreated paranoid schizophrenia for years.

Some neighbors said they had been afraid, but no one wanted to "get involved." This sparked a public debate in Australia about mental health, taboos, and government failure. Why had no one helped? Why had no one intervened?

In the wake of this debate, a fund was set up in 2021: a support program for Indigenous families affected by mental illness. Initiated by the victims' grandfather, Rod Villi, it was intended not only to provide financial assistance but also to enable education and early detection. Villi explained in an interview, "We can't change the past. But we can make sure that something like this never happens again."

Her son Lewis now lives a secluded life. He and his sister Norina share the invisible legacy of this tragedy, a memory that never fades. In one of his rare interviews, Lewis explained, "We all carry them with us. Their voices, their laughter. We are the last ones left, and the first ones to miss them." The tattoo on his arm is not just a symbol, but a promise: that life goes on and the memory remains.

Today, years later, Australia still remembers the Cairns incident. It is not only the story of a mother who became a perpetrator due to a serious illness, but also the story of a society that looked away for too long. The question remains: could the tragedy have been prevented? And how many Thaidays are there still, untreated, overwhelmed, alone?

The Thaiday case sparked debates, changed laws, and initiated support programs. But above all, it did one thing: it engraved eight names in the collective memory. Eight innocent children whose lives ended brutally, and whose memory could save the lives of many others today.

Watch the video

A profiler's opinion on this case

CASE 20

20. DECEMBER

On December 20, 1996, Julie Busken was supposed to drive home. It was the morning before Christmas, and her parents were already on their way to Norman, Oklahoma, USA, to pick up their only daughter. Julie had celebrated her university graduation the day before. After four years of study, she was ready to return to Arkansas, back to the small town of Benton, where she wanted to open her own dance studio, but on that frosty morning, everything was about to change.

Shortly after sunrise, around 5:30 a.m., a resident of the apartment complex where Julie lived heard a shrill scream. He woke up with a start and looked out the window, but the street was empty. No movement, no struggle, no sign of anyone. Unsure, he called the police. A patrol car arrived a short time later, drove around the building, and shone flashlights into dark corners, but they found nothing suspicious; no crime scene, no victim. The officers noted the incident and drove away.

Hours later, around 11 a.m., Ryan, Julie's boyfriend and colleague, knocked on her door. They had arranged to meet for a farewell breakfast, only Julie wasn't there. Her car, a red Mitsubishi Eclipse, was also missing. Ryan waited, knocked again, but then went to work. Maybe she was out, he thought. Maybe something had changed, but in the afternoon, after work, he was back at the door. The car was still gone, and Julie remained missing.

What no one knew at the time was that Julie was already dead. Her abduction had probably taken place at the very moment she had come home in the first light of dawn, right in front of her apartment.

Towards evening, a couple reported to the police. The man had been walking by a remote lake at noon, about a 15-minute drive from the apartment complex. Something in the water had caught his attention, a dark silhouette, motionless, only half visible. It was only when his wife later returned with him to examine the spot that they realized it could be a body.

A short time later, their suspicion was confirmed. The police recovered the body of a young woman from the water, bound, with a gunshot wound to the head. Her jeans were open, her clothes had slipped. The dead woman had no identification on her, but investigators found a jacket nearby. Inside was a name: Julie.

The discovery at the lake put investigators on high alert. That same evening, forensic specialists arrived, and the area was cordoned off, with every inch of the shore systematically examined. Near the spot where Julie's body had been floating in the water, they discovered two sets of footprints in the sand: smaller ones, presumably from a woman, and larger, deeper ones. Both led to the water, but only the larger footprints returned. The conclusion was gruesome: the perpetrator had led Julie to the shore, shot her, thrown her into the water, and returned alone.

A short time later, it was confirmed by the medical examiner that the dead woman was indeed Julie Busken. The cause of death: a shot to the back of the head at close range. Her hands were tied with a shoelace, her clothing showed signs of sexual abuse, and forensic scientists found traces of semen in the fibers of her jacket. A DNA sample was taken, but in 1996, the national DNA database system was still in its infancy. It was not possible to find an immediate match with a perpetrator profile.

Julie's parents, who had meanwhile arrived in Norman, learned of their daughter's murder that same day. They had come to help her pack, and instead heard of her murder; their world fell apart. Their daughter, 21 years old, intelligent, determined, full of plans, had been brutally torn from life.

The investigation initially focused on Julie's immediate circle. Friends, colleagues, neighbors, everyone was questioned. Particularly relevant: the early morning emergency call and the statements of two witnesses. A police officer who lived nearby had also heard the scream, went outside, but saw nothing. However, another neighbor reported something far more sinister: he heard the scream and then a male voice saying, "Shut up and get in the car." Then the sound of two car doors slamming, before silence.

A woman reported seeing a red Mitsubishi Eclipse that morning. A man was sitting at the wheel, next to him a young woman, she looked frightened, while the man appeared tense and irritable. Another witness saw the same car later near the lake; he also noticed the driver's behavior. Both witnesses independently provided a description of the man. This resulted in a composite sketch—the only image of the alleged perpetrator ever presented to the public.

Julie had probably been abducted right in front of her apartment, in the middle of a residential area, within sight of her neighbors, but no one had seen anything. It was one of those brutal seconds when violence crept into normality and disappeared before anyone can react.

The police searched frantically for Julie's car, a red Mitsubishi Eclipse. They suspected that the perpetrator had used it for the kidnapping. It had not been reported stolen, had not ended up in a tow yard, and had not been found abandoned. It was only days later that an officer discovered it in a parking lot directly opposite Julie's apartment building. It had never been far away, just well hidden. The killer had brought it back there, almost as if he wanted to leave a mark.

In the car, investigators found Julie's pajama pants, which also had traces of semen on them. Under the driver's seat was sand, most likely from the lake shore. The crime had left traces, but no name, fingerprints, or camera footage. The perpetrator seemed like a phantom, but the investigators were certain: he had been closer to Julie than anyone thought.

After finding the car and the traces inside it, the investigators began to systematically comb through the area. Who had seen Julie? Who had spoken to her? Who could have followed her? Her last hours were well documented: the farewell party with friends, the late-night snack with her roommate, everything fit together, but what exactly happened between 5:00 a.m. and the scream at 5:30 a.m. remained a black hole.

The investigators hoped to find clues in the neighborhood. They questioned dozens of neighbors. Some had heard noise, others thought they had seen a red car, but nothing was concrete enough to provide a hot lead. Only a detailed analysis of the shoe prints on the lake shore yielded an interesting finding: the prints came from a Nike model, Air 242, size 9. The police contacted Nike directly and received confirmation: it was a rather rare model that had only been produced in limited quantities, but that was all they could find out. The clues remained inconclusive.

The DNA samples found on Julie also failed to provide any clarity at first. Investigators tested more than 200 men, friends, colleagues, fellow students, neighbors, but none of them matched. No one was the perpetrator; there was no DNA match. The clues led nowhere.

In the months that followed, the case was reviewed again and again. The investigators kept at it, but time was working against them. Eventually, the file was set aside. Julie was not forgotten, but her story became one of many unsolved cases.

It was not until four and a half years later that the investigation gained momentum. A woman contacted the police; she was in prison for theft. There she had seen the composite sketch from the case, and it reminded her of someone: a young man named Denis, with whom she had had contact in the past. The investigators pricked up their ears. At the time of the crime, Denis had lived only a few streets away from Julie's apartment. He was 23 years old at the time, and his facial features did indeed match the sketch.

The police spoke to him, but Denis refused to cooperate. He refused to answer questions and did not want to provide a DNA sample, but a court forced him to do so. When the laboratory analyzed the sample, the next surprise followed: it wasn't Denis, but his DNA was genetically similar to that of the perpetrator, almost like that of a close relative.

The investigators immediately checked Denis' family. He had only one brother, and his DNA was also tested; also negative. So, it was clear that neither man was the perpetrator, but they were related to him. This discovery gave the investigators hope, but it led nowhere. There was no third brother, or other known male relatives, so this lead also came to nothing.

The case was handed over to the cold case department. The years passed, and hope became routine, then resignation. Julie's killer was still at large until, in the summer of 2004, the investigation team received a phone call that changed everything. In July 2004, almost eight years after the murder, an FBI agent contacted the investigators in charge. A match had been found in the national DNA database CODIS, and it matched exactly with the sample secured in the Julie Busken case in 1996. The name: Anthony Sanchez.

Sanchez was no stranger to the authorities. In 2002, he had been arrested for kidnapping, sexual assault, and armed robbery. When he was arrested, a DNA sample had been taken from him, as is standard procedure. At the time, the sample was simply entered into the database for safekeeping. Now, two years later, the circle was complete.

Investigators immediately traveled to the prison where Sanchez was being held. They wanted a direct comparison, not only with the old sample from CODIS, but again with the original material from Julie's case. The result: a perfect match.

When investigators investigated Sanchez's past, they found something shocking. At the time of the crime, he lived only about a mile from Julie's apartment. He had a long history of violence, burglary, and drug abuse. His girlfriend at the time reported that in December 1996, he owned a pair of Nike shoes, the same model whose prints had been found on the lake shore: Air 242, size 9; she herself had been given an identical pair by him. In her diary from that time, there was even an entry confirming this purchase.

Another ex-girlfriend provided a detail that sounded grotesque at first, but proved to be decisive: she reported that Anthony and his father regularly shot at the walls of the house with guns, often under the influence of drugs. The investigators applied for a search warrant for the father's house at the time. In one of the walls, they found a bullet of the same caliber as the bullet that had killed Julie, a .22 caliber.

Ballistic analysis revealed that both bullets came from a rare weapon. Although it could not be proven with 100% certainty that it was the same gun, the notches on the bullets matched strikingly. This was another piece of the puzzle in the picture of a perpetrator that was slowly but surely becoming clearer.

Then they rechecked the strange calls that had been made from Julie's cell phone on the night of the crime. One was to a weather service, but the second call went to a non-existent number. Investigators discovered that this number differed by only one digit from the phone number of Sanchez's girlfriend at the time. The perpetrator had probably tried to dial it from memory and made a mistake.

These details, together with the DNA match and the shoe prints, were enough to officially charge Anthony Sanchez with the murder of Julie Busken, but when confronted with this, he denied any involvement. He said he had never seen Julie, never known her. His lawyers tried to cast doubt on the case. The DNA sample might have been contaminated. His fingerprints were not found in the car. That was not enough for a conviction.

The experts disagreed; the DNA match was clear, and the probability of it being a mistake was 1 in 94 billion.

During the trial, the prosecution presented a consistent overall picture: Sanchez had kidnapped, sexually abused, murdered, and thrown the victim into the lake. The forensic evidence, witness statements, DNA, shoe prints, and even the curiosity of the wrong number dialed painted a clear picture. The jury unanimously found him guilty.

The sentence was quickly decided. In the state of Oklahoma, first-degree murder with sexual motive and intent meant the death penalty, but the case was not over yet. Although the verdict had been handed down, Sanchez tried everything he could to appeal it in the years that followed.

After the guilty verdict, Anthony Sanchez immediately began a series of appeals, but all of them were rejected. The evidence was clear; there was no doubt about the DNA match, and the 1996 composite sketch matched his appearance at the time remarkably well.

Years later, as the execution date approached, Sanchez changed his strategy. He began to claim that it was not he, but his father, who was the real perpetrator. The man, he said, had once confessed to him under the influence of alcohol and drugs that he had "killed a girl" near the lake.

The claim came late. His father was now dead, having taken his own life in 2006. The story spread quickly in the media, and anti-death penalty activists picked up on it. To many, it sounded plausible: a young man from a violent, unstable home who was made a scapegoat, while the real perpetrator was long dead.

However, the facts remained, and the prosecution stated that even if Sanchez's father had killed Julie Busken, the DNA trace on her clothing could never be a complete match with Sanchez's DNA. This is because genetic relatedness provides similarities, but not identity. The probability of a complete match between father and son is zero.

The presiding judge also strongly disagreed with the theory. He publicly stated that this narrative did not provide any new evidence and served only to delegitimize the conviction. The scientific facts left no room for doubt: Anthony Sanchez was the perpetrator.

Nevertheless, Sanchez received support. A former girlfriend of his father suddenly came forward. She claimed that the father had confessed to her several times that he had "killed a young girl" and that he had never spoken about it out of fear, but her statement came many years after his death, and there was no evidence; no details, no clues, and no independent witnesses.

Some saw this as a last-ditch attempt to prevent the execution. A former prosecutor spoke publicly of a "staged story," which is not uncommon in death penalty cases: the blame is shifted to someone already dead to exonerate the convicted person, even if there is no evidence.

In 2015, a real opportunity seemed to open up for Sanchez. The state of Oklahoma imposed a moratorium on all executions. Technical glitches in previous executions had led to international criticism. During this period of postponement, Sanchez and his supporters found new hope: a petition was launched, collecting more than 10,000 signatures. Numerous media outlets reported on the case, with some articles even portraying it as a possible miscarriage of justice.

But in 2021, the moratorium was lifted and Oklahoma resumed executions, and Sanchez's execution became more likely again. A state clemency committee set a new hearing date. It was his last chance to escape death via the direct route of clemency, but then something unexpected happened: Sanchez refused to attend the hearing.

He said he did not believe in clemency. Over the years, he had seen prisoners go into such hearings full of hope and still end up being executed. He had decided to "stop giving himself false hope." That is why he voluntarily gave up the chance to appear before the clemency board. This decision raised many questions.

Because if Sanchez was indeed innocent, why did he reject his only real chance of salvation? Why did he voluntarily give up his last chance to escape his death sentence?

However, many people believed he was guilty. Even Julie's parents, who had remained silent all these years, now spoke out publicly. They said they had never believed his story. For them, it was clear: Anthony Sanchez was their daughter's murderer, and the guilty verdict was justified.

In October 2023, the date for Sanchez's execution was finally set. The state of Oklahoma announced that the execution would take place on September 21, 2023. In the weeks leading up to it, media outlets across the country revisited the case. Many warned of a possible miscarriage of justice, while others pointed to the overwhelming evidence that had led to the conviction.

On the day of the execution, the Oklahoma State Penitentiary in McAlester was surrounded by protesters. On one side were opponents of the death penalty, on the other were supporters of Julie's family. The tension was palpable, unlike in almost any other case in recent years.

Sanchez himself showed no emotion. In his final statement, he said he was "innocent" and would "take the truth to his grave." He declined both a final prayer and a final conversation with a chaplain and did not ask for forgiveness. At 10:19 a.m. local time, the lethal injection was administered, and at 10:25 a.m., Anthony Sanchez was dead.

For Julie's parents, it was not a day of revenge. They later said that they felt no satisfaction, only silence. A sense of closure. Not victory, but closure. The pain will never go away, but perhaps healing can now begin. In an interview, Julie's mother said:

"It was her dream to start her own studio and teach children to dance. She would have had a wonderful life. Not only was her future taken from her – it changed all of us."

Today, a simple memorial on the university campus commemorates Julie. There, where she studied, dreamed, laughed, and danced.

Watch the video

A profiler's opinion on this case

CASE 21

21. DECEMBER

On December 21, 2019, a decision was made in Bolivia that would cost dozens of people their lives. In a small office, Dr. Freddie Timme issued a medical certificate, a piece of paper that seemed harmless but would have devastating consequences. It certified that a convicted murderer had a number of illnesses: hepatomegaly, gastritis, diabetes, stomach ulcers, asthma, and even a supposedly life-threatening liver disease. The patient: Richard Choque Flores, convicted of kidnapping, rape, and murder. The certificate recommended his release on health grounds. Three days later, shortly before Christmas, a judge accepted the bribe: $3,500 in cash and a bottle of whiskey, and the murderer was free again.

No one could have guessed at the time that the most dangerous sex offender in recent Bolivian history was being released back into society, and no one knew how many lives this decision would cost.

Choque Flores' story did not begin on that December day. The serial killer had already left his first bloody traces years earlier. He was born in 1988 in El Alto, a city above La Paz, at an altitude of over 4,000 meters. His father was a police officer, his mother a teacher; a seemingly ordinary family. But when Choque Flores was four years old, his father was shot and killed while on duty, and this early trauma shaped him. He withdrew, began to show signs of abnormality, hardly spoke, and avoided other children. His mother tried to control him, but the facade of normality was already beginning to crumble.

As a teenager, Choque Flores attended a military school, but soon dropped out. He returned to the house he shared with his mother and sister, and there he transformed into something dark without anyone noticing. His social contacts were sparse, his behavior increasingly manipulative. He began spending time in online forums, assuming false identities, offering help, and taking advantage of every moment someone trusted him.

The case of his younger cousin Fidel was particularly tragic. When Fidel wanted to apply to military school in 2011, Choque Flores promised to help him in exchange for a payment of $5,000. Fidel said goodbye to his mother, met with Choque Flores, and disappeared without a trace. Years later, it would emerge that he was one of the first victims.

The list grew. In November 2013, law student Blanca Rubili Machi disappeared after meeting with a supposed university instructor, also Choque Flores under a false name. Days later, her body was found buried in a sack. Choque Flores was arrested and, in 2015, sentenced to thirty years in prison without parole.

Yet, on December 24, 2019, with a forged medical certificate and some cash, he was back on the streets.

He returned to his family home, the very place where so many of his crimes had taken place. The neighbors had no idea, and Choque Flores began killing again.

No sooner was he free, Richard Choque Flores wasted no time. His methods were now more sophisticated, but the pattern remained the same: he used social networks to target young women in precarious life situations. He created fake profiles, sometimes as an attractive young man, sometimes as a police officer, often under female names. He particularly often used the profile of a supposed woman named Haida Miitsi. Under this name, he posted tempting job offers in Facebook groups: escort services, courier jobs, promotional jobs, all with the promise of quick money.

His preferred hunting ground was La Paz, and in particular, his hometown of El Alto, where many people live in poverty and young women are often forced to seize every opportunity. The scam was perfidious: as soon as a woman responded,

Richard Choque Flores arranged a personal meeting. There was no job opportunity waiting for her; instead, it was a prepared ambush.

The tactic he used to lure them into the trap was particularly perfidious. In some cases, he pretended to be conducting a police raid: he deliberately placed substances in a room he had rented beforehand, then showed up in a police uniform and threatened the women with arrest unless they cooperated. In his vocabulary, "cooperation" meant sexual violence, blackmail, video recordings, and ransom demands to the victims' families.

On May 17, 2021, 17-year-old Lucy Maya Ramirez disappeared. She had previously responded to an offer in a Facebook group apparently posted by Haida Miitsi. The next day, her mother received a message: $70,000 in ransom or her daughter would die. The message contained explicit images that made it clear how serious the threat was. The family had no way of raising such a sum.

Just three months later, on August 27, 2021, history repeated itself. Fifteen-year-old Iris Maylin Wilka disappeared under similar circumstances. Again, a ransom demand was received, again for $70,000, again accompanied by images.

Meanwhile, other women also contacted the police. They reported a man who had deceived them on social media, then abused and threatened them, but for a long time, no one realized that a single perpetrator was behind all these cases; the same man who was supposed to still be in prison.

It wasn't until early 2022 that the investigation gained momentum. A 43-year-old woman reported to the police that she had been attacked by a man who had offered her a job on Facebook. She managed to escape and reported the man to the police. This statement led to the decisive breakthrough.

The police arrested Richard Choque Flores in a hotel on January 24, 2022. What followed shook not only Bolivia, but it was the beginning of a scandal that called an entire justice system into question.

After Richard Choque Flores' arrest on January 24, 2022, investigators immediately searched his home in El Alto. What they found there was beyond imagination: in a hidden area of the garden, they came across two shallow graves. In one of them, they discovered the body of Lucy Maya Ramirez, and in the other, the remains of Iris Maylin Wilka. Both girls had been bound, abused, and wrapped in sacks. For the families, it was the cruel confirmation of their worst fears, and for the investigators, a shock that shook the entire country.

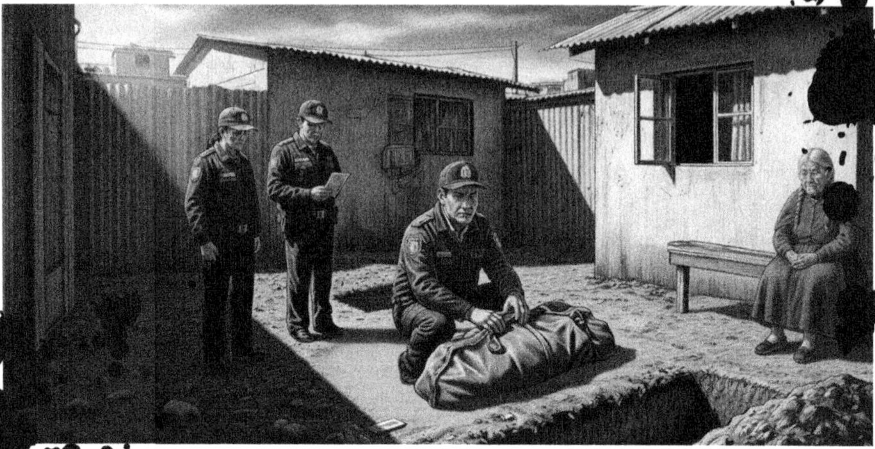

That wasn't all, though. As they continued to search the house, they stumbled upon the solution to a case that had been considered unsolved for years: the disappearance of Fidel, Choque Flores' cousin, who had set off in 2011 with the dream of studying at a military academy. Investigators found his skeleton under a thin layer of earth, buried in the same garden, just a few meters away from the girls.

For eleven years, he had remained silent while his aunt desperately searched for answers. Now she had the bitter certainty: her nephew had killed her son.

These findings exceeded all previous assumptions, but it didn't stop with these three victims. The police discovered dozens of copies of ID cards, women's personal belongings, and even clothing that had apparently been kept as trophies in the house where Choque Flores lived. Over the next few weeks, the authorities received more than 70 reports from women who claimed to have been harassed, threatened, raped, or blackmailed by Choque Flores. The number of unreported cases could be even higher. Many victims had remained silent for fear of reprisals, but now the silence had been broken.

The system that should have stopped him had instead let him back on the streets, and there he had continued, more ruthless, more calculating. By now, it was clear:

the case of Richard Choque Flores was more than an isolated incident. He was a symbol of a failed justice system that had made itself complicit through corruption and indifference.

How was it possible that a murderer sentenced to 30 years in prison was released even though there was no medical necessity?

The answer was as shocking as the crimes themselves, and it would come to light in the next phase of the investigation.

The answer to this question was not long in coming, and it shook Bolivia to its core. The investigation revealed that Choque Flores' lawyers had filed a momentous motion with the court on December 21, 2019. They claimed that their client was seriously ill and could not survive under prison conditions.

Choque Flores returned to his childhood home, to his mother and sister, who either had no idea or willingly turned a blind eye. What followed was a second wave of horror. Instead of keeping quiet, as a man who had narrowly escaped death in prison would do, Choque Flores immediately resumed his old ways. Even more sophisticated, even more ruthless.

What no one knew was that Choque Flores had long since compiled a new list of potential victims. A list that included girls who had never responded to him, and who survived only by chance.

His luck ran out when one of his victims decided not to remain silent, and that marked the beginning of the end.

Photos of the girls he had abused circulated on social media, accompanied by hashtags such as #JusticiaParaLucy ("Justice for Lucy"), #NiUnaMenos ("Not one less"), and #ElAltoNoOlvida ("El Alto does not forget"). Thousands shared their anger.

On January 31, 2022, thousands of women marched through the streets of La Paz and El Alto. They carried photos of the victims and posters reading "You let him go for money" and "Our lives are worth more." The protests spread to other cities like Cochabamba, Santa Cruz, and Oruro. It was more than anger; it was a revolt against a system that ignored poverty, inequality, and women's voices.

It wasn't just the justice system that came under fire. In the days following the arrest, anger was also directed at the perpetrator's family. After his release, Choque Flores had moved in with his mother and sister. These two women had lived with him all this time and remained silent. Neighbors reported that they had repeatedly heard suspicious noises, that packages had been delivered and taken away, that girls had entered the house, and never come out again.

When it was confirmed that the mother and sister were most likely accomplices, angry riots broke out. The family's house in El Alto was smeared with red paint and the word "CÓMPLICES" (accomplices). Windows were smashed. The police had to secure the building and eventually arrest the two women themselves.

What remained was a nation in shock, but no longer silent. Women's organizations, lawyers, journalists, and politicians resolutely demanded a far-reaching reform of the justice system. The fact that a serial killer could only gain his freedom through bribery must never happen again. The judge who abused his power and made this possible was dismissed from office without notice.

Watch the video

A profiler's opinion on this case

CASE 22

22. DECEMBER

On December 22, 1990, the Tiede family set off on their way back to their mountain cabin in snow-covered Weber Canyon in Utah, USA. Christmas was just around the corner, and like every year, they wanted to spend the holidays in their secluded, cozy cabin, far away from the hustle and bustle of everyday life, surrounded by snow, mountains, and family. As they did every year, they looked forward to riding snowmobiles together through the snow-covered landscape and enjoying the quiet, wintry nature to the fullest. Nineteen-year-old Linae Tiede was traveling with her mother, Kaye, and her grandmother, Beth Potts, to decorate the house for the holidays. Stockings were already hanging above the fireplace, an icy wind was blowing outside, and soon the familiar voices and laughter of family and friends would be heard inside the cabin.

What they didn't know was that two men had already gained access to the cabin: 25-year-old Lester Taylor and 21-year-old Edward Steven Deli. Both men had been released from prison on parole just a week earlier, and instead of taking up employment as required, they had hidden in the mountains. There, they broke into empty cabins and eventually spent the night in the Tiede family's cabin. In a phone call, Taylor had even announced that he wanted to wait for the residents to return so he could steal their vehicle.

The family's return was uneventful at first. Kaye, Beth, and Linae fought their way through heavy snowfall to the cabin. Linae peered through the kitchen window and noticed movement behind the refrigerator, but she didn't think anything of it. Perhaps it was her cousin who wanted to surprise them. But when Linae entered, a man she didn't know, with curly hair and a gray hoodie, emerged from the shadows and pointed a gun at her. Seconds later, Kaye and Beth were confronted by a second armed man in the hallway.

Kaye, terrified, tried to negotiate. She offered the men everything they wanted, but before she could finish her sentence, Taylor pulled the trigger twice without warning. Kaye fell to the floor, fatally wounded. Linae had to watch helplessly as her mother died. When she turned around, she saw her grandmother being shot in the head; blood covered the floor. For Linae, it all felt surreal, as if she were in a nightmare from which she would wake up at any moment.

But the horror had only just begun.

While Linae was still trying to process the shock, she heard one of the family's snowmobiles; her father, Rolf, and her younger sister, Tricia, were approaching the cabin. Still in shock, but filled with the will to survive, Linae thought quickly. She had to warn them, or at least buy some time, but before she could react, Taylor grabbed her and led her to the garage at gunpoint. There, she was to show him where the car keys were. At that very moment, Rolf and Tricia arrived.

One of the men, now wearing a ski mask, jumped out of the house and pointed his gun at the father and daughter. He ordered them to come into the house immediately. When Rolf saw his daughter, he suspected the worst. Her tear-stained eyes, her trembling body, this could not be a harmless incident. He obeyed silently and without resistance. Inside the house, the perpetrators demanded money. Rolf took everything out of his pockets and threw it on the floor, but Taylor gave the order to shoot him. The first shot clicked into thin air. The gun misfired. The second attempt also failed, but on the third try, the bullet crashed through Rolf's face. He slumped to the ground.

Linae thought her father was dead, too. Three loved ones, wiped out in a matter of minutes. The stench of blood and gasoline hung in the air. Everything was eerily quiet, and yet Linae had no time for grief. The perpetrators apparently planned to set the house on fire to cover their tracks. There were several gasoline cans for the snowmobiles stored in the cabin, a fortunate circumstance for Taylor. He spread gasoline on the upper floor, and shortly thereafter, the fire alarm sounded. The fire ate through the walls while Taylor and Deli fled with their hostages.

Linae and Tricia were forced to drive the snowmobiles, and Taylor and Deli sat behind them. The girls thought they would be killed as soon as they reached their destination, the family car, but then, out of nowhere, a relative appeared: their uncle Randy. He waved to them, unaware, and the sisters didn't dare warn him. One wrong look, one careless attempt, and he too could die. So, they drove on.

But Randy became suspicious. Why were his nieces ignoring him? Why did they seem so tense? Why was there another person sitting on each of the snowmobiles? He drove to the parking lot where the family's cars were usually parked. Just as he arrived, he saw a man without a coat or gloves, completely hypothermic, who could barely get off the snowmobile, his brother Rolf.

Unbelievable but true: Rolf had survived the gunshot to the head. While the perpetrators fled with the girls, he had pretended to be dead, later dragged himself to the bathroom, torn the burning clothes from his body, and extinguished the flames in the shower. Then, driven by desperation and fear for his daughters, he drove after them despite his serious injuries.

Now he was here, bleeding, semi-conscious, but alive. Randy was shocked when he saw his brother in this condition: his face swollen, his chin bloody, his gaze blurred, but Rolf could speak, and he said only one thing:

"They have Linae and Tricia." There was no time to lose. Randy helped Rolf into the back seat of his car, jumped behind the wheel, and drove off. Fortunately, his car, a rare luxury at the time, had a built-in car phone. Randy immediately tried to call the emergency number, but the reception was poor, and the connection kept breaking.

Nevertheless, Randy didn't give up and was able to reach the police. While driving, he described the situation, the perpetrators, and the vehicle to the police. Then he lost the connection again. Without hesitation, he drove to the nearest gas station, ran to the phone booth, and made another emergency call. The information was now complete: two armed men with hostages, traveling in a silver Lincoln. The Summit County police responded immediately.

Meanwhile, Linae and Tricia were still on the road with their kidnappers. Taylor and Deli had forced them to get into the family car. The girls sat in the back, next to each other, their minds racing. Tricia noticed that one of the perpetrators had put his gun in the trunk. Hope? Maybe, but the men were vigilant. One of them suddenly pulled out a knife he had hidden in his coat pocket as if he had read their minds.

At the same time, Randy was racing after the route the perpetrators had presumably taken with the seriously injured Rolf. Then, suddenly, in the distance, the vehicle they were looking for appeared. Randy got closer. The police were already on their way, but it took minutes that felt like an eternity. Randy considered forcing the car off the road, but he decided against it because his nieces could die in the maneuver.

Finally, sirens in the distance. The police had arrived, and what followed was a nerve-wracking chase through the snow-covered streets. The Lincoln skidded across the road, trying to swerve, but then, a mistake. The perpetrators lost control, the vehicle crashed down an embankment, and came to rest on its side.

The silence that followed was eerie.

Then, movement. Two figures climbed out of the car: it was Linae and Tricia. They raised their hands, trembling, and shouted that they were hostages. The officers immediately drew their weapons, surrounded the car, and called on the perpetrators to surrender. Taylor and Deli had no choice. They were arrested without resistance, but also without a hint of remorse.

The girls, exhausted, traumatized, and completely broken, collapsed. One of the officers approached them, gently placed a blanket over their shoulders, and said the words they had dared not believe: "Your father is alive."

For a moment, Linae and Tricia thought they had misheard. Their father? Alive? Just a few hours earlier, they had watched as he was shot in the face. How he collapsed. How he lay motionless on the floor. That he had survived seemed like a miracle, a miracle that, for a moment, took away the horror they had experienced.

In the hours after Taylor and Deli's arrest, the investigation began at the scene of the crime. The police found a scene of horror: blood on the wooden floorboards, charred remains, the smell of burnt hair and burnt clothing in the air. The once cozy vacation home of the Tiede family had become a crime scene that looked like a scene from a horror movie.

In the living room, the carpet was soaked with blood, and in the garage, a large pool of blood had formed, which had already frozen due to the sub-zero temperatures. Investigators secured evidence, collected clues, and documented every detail. One of the officers even discovered a video camera that had been set up in the house. On the tape: footage of Taylor opening Christmas presents and Deli laughing beside him; a cruel testament to their disrespect for the family's suffering.

Linae and Tricia were taken to safety, given medical attention, and questioned. Despite everything, they showed remarkable composure. Still too dazed to fully comprehend reality, they soberly described what had happened, the movements of the perpetrators, the sequence of events, every little detail. Their statements would later play a central role in court.

Meanwhile, Rolf was fighting for his life in the hospital. The shot to the head had disfigured his face, and the fire burned his body, but he had survived because he knew his daughters needed him. Even before the smoke had completely cleared, he had tried to get up, torn off his clothes, extinguished the fire, and set off. It wasn't just a will to survive; it was love. Nothing else had driven him down the mountain.

When Linae and Tricia learned that their father was seriously injured but out of danger, they fell into each other's arms. The house that had once been a place of warmth and security for them was destroyed. Their mother and grandmother, murdered. Their father, scarred for life, but they were alive, and they were together.

The investigators now faced a difficult task: What role had each perpetrator played? Who had fired the shots? Who had planned it? Who had hesitated? Linae was convinced that both men were equally guilty, that neither was less to blame than the other, and she was prepared to testify to that in court.

The justice system began with what is often the most difficult thing for many relatives of victims: the lengthy, often sobering journey through a court case. For Linae and Tricia, it meant facing the horror again in the form of witness statements, photos, crime scene recordings, and meeting the perpetrators themselves once more.

Five months after the attack, Lester Taylor pleaded guilty to double murder. It was a calculated move: in return, the state dropped several other charges, including attempted murder, kidnapping, and arson. During the trial, Taylor claimed he couldn't remember many details, as if his memory had been erased, but the evidence spoke for itself. The girls' statements, the videotapes, the evidence in the house, everything painted a picture of a cold-blooded, controlled perpetrator. The court sentenced him to death for both murders.

Taylor showed no remorse. No emotion when the verdict was announced. No glance at the survivors. He remained silent, closed off, as if frozen. Tricia and Linae held each other tight; they knew that this was only the first step and that the second would follow.

A few weeks later, the trial of Edward Steven Deli began. Unlike Taylor, Deli was not charged with first-degree murder, but with second-degree murder, a decision based primarily on doubts about his direct involvement in the crime. The court sentenced him to life imprisonment with the possibility of parole after 62 years at the earliest. This means that Deli could be released in 2063 at the earliest. However, the judge recommended that this possibility not be considered later, with the result that Deli would have to spend the rest of his life in prison.

Particularly traumatic for Linae was a moment during the trial that she would never forget: she was asked to hold the murder weapon that had been used to kill her mother and grandmother. It was humiliating, but she endured it with stoic calm. She showed where the perpetrator had stood, how he had held the weapon, and described what had happened in those moments. Her strength impressed not only the court but also the public.

When Rolf Tiede entered the courtroom, severely scarred but alive, Deli froze. It was the moment when the perpetrators realized that they had not only failed, but their victim was standing before them, ready to tell the truth.

Linae and Tricia now knew that they had won, not only in court, but as human beings, and they vowed that they would never stop fighting to honor their family's legacy.

In 2001, more than a decade after the crime, Edward Steven Deli wrote a letter to the Tiede family. In it, he again confessed his guilt, but claimed he had not planned the murders. He had only wanted to rob cabins, but Taylor had had other intentions. After Kaye and Beth's deaths, he wrote, it was too late. He had accepted what had happened and simply moved on. It was a letter that oscillated between remorse and excuses.

It took Linae nine years to respond. Her words were calm, clear, and unrelenting. She wrote that she forgave him, but she immediately made it clear that forgiveness did not mean forgetting, and she would never forget.

Despite everything, Tricia and Linae led fulfilling lives. Tricia became the mother of two children and said that that terrible day in December had not broken her, but shaped her. She was no longer the girl she had been back then, but a woman who had survived and loved.

After a failed marriage, Linae married her childhood friend Nathan. Together they raised nine children. She continued to believe in the good in people, not naively, but consciously, because she knew how precious peace is.

Rolf, her father, not only survived the massacre but fought his way back to life. He rebuilt the burned-down hut with his own hands. The family met every year at Christmas at this very place. Where horror had once reigned, they created a new beginning. For Linae and Tricia, the hut was a sacred place, filled with memories, but also with hope. They believed that the souls of their mother and grandmother still watched over them there.

In 2008, Rolf Tiede died of cancer, surrounded by his family. He had lived a full life, full of pride in his daughters and grandchildren.

Three days after Christmas 1990, Beth and Kaye were buried, and yet, almost thirty years later, something of them remained alive: in every story that was told, in every tear that was shed, and in every laugh that rang out in the new old cabin.

Watch the video

A profiler's opinion on this case

CASE

23

23. DECEMBER

December 23, 1996. An eerie silence hung over a remote house near the small Irish village of Toormore that day. It was the day before Christmas Eve, yet the coastal landscape of West Cork was not enveloped in festive tranquility, but something else, something intangible, yet palpable. On that day, a neighbor reported a disturbing observation: the front door of the white country house, which belonged to a French producer, was wide open. No one answered when they knocked. No lights, no music, no smoke from the chimney. Only the wind whistling through the trees. The police were notified, and when the officers arrived at the house, they did not yet know that they were at the beginning of a story that would occupy Ireland for decades.

The next morning, a woman's body was discovered on a dirt road, just a few meters from the house. She was wearing a blue bathrobe, pajama pants, and heavy boots. Her face was barely recognizable. It later transpired that the woman was Sophie Toscan du Plantier, a 39-year-old documentary filmmaker from France. She had bought a holiday home in Ireland to write in peace and quiet and get away from the hustle and bustle of Paris. No one could explain why she had left the house in her pajama bottoms that night, or whether she had left of her own accord.

Sophie had traveled alone. Her husband, Daniel Toscan du Plantier, a prominent French film producer, had stayed in Paris. Her neighbors described her as polite, reserved, and naturally elegant. The small community in Toormore, where everyone knows everyone else, was deeply shaken by the brutal violence of the crime. It was a murder unlike anything this place had ever seen before.

The investigation began immediately, but it soon became apparent that solving this crime would be anything but easy. There were no obvious signs of a break-in, no motive, no suspects. What they had was a crime scene in a remote area, a badly disfigured body, and many unanswered questions.

What no one could have guessed was that the murder of Sophie Toscan du Plantier would become one of the most mysterious and controversial criminal cases in Irish history, and the truth would not be easy to find.

The investigation into the Sophie Toscan du Plantier case began under the most difficult conditions. The weather was harsh, the crime scene was unprotected, and the first traces may already have been blurred by rain and wind. The West Cork police were dealing with an extraordinary crime, not only because of the brutality of the act, but also because of the international attention the case attracted. Sophie was no stranger: as the wife of a famous French film producer, her death immediately became a political issue, both in France and in Ireland. For the police, it was a gauntlet of circumstantial evidence, allegations, and a community in a case that had suddenly become one of international interest.

A name emerged in the early days: Ian Bailey. A British journalist who not only knew a striking amount about the crime, but also made contradictory statements. But Bailey was more than just a curious observer; he was one of the first on the scene, one of the first to speak to colleagues from the press, and repeatedly emphasized how shocked he was. The Briton lived with his partner Jules Thomas near the scene of the crime, worked as a freelance journalist and author, published poems, and, as many later noted, was astonishingly quick to provide information. He reported on the murder for British and Irish newspapers, wrote articles, and conducted interviews, often in such detail that the police became suspicious.

Bailey had no alibi witnesses for the night of the crime. He claimed to have spent the night at home, but his partner could not confirm his whereabouts during the critical hours. In addition, several neighbors reported that Bailey had scratches on his hands and arms in the days after the murder, allegedly from cutting down a fir tree, but the police doubted this version. Things became even more suspicious when Bailey began to entangle himself in contradictory statements. At one point, he said he had seen the woman before, and later he claimed he had never known the victim personally.

Investigators began to watch Bailey more closely. They tapped his phone, searched his house, and questioned him several times, but they had a problem: there was no hard evidence. No DNA, no fingerprints, no witnesses who had seen him near the scene of the crime. Bailey repeatedly protested his innocence, but his behavior, his demeanor, and his sometimes arrogant manner made him the target of public suspicion.

In the background, Sophie's family fought for answers. Her parents and husband were appalled by the slowness and indecisiveness of the Irish authorities. They demanded justice and demanded an indictment, but the authorities hesitated. There was not enough evidence to press charges, and there was too much suspicion to acquit him.

Meanwhile, Ian Bailey continued to live in West Cork, unmolested, but under close observation. He was a free man, but known everywhere as a suspected murderer. And so the story began to change: from the brutal murder of a woman to a criminal case that would soon become a national trauma.

While no official charges were brought against Ian Bailey in Ireland, pressure on the authorities grew in France. Sophie's family fought tirelessly to keep the case from being forgotten. For them, it was clear: Bailey was the perpetrator. Too many clues, too many strange statements, too many odd coincidences.

In the years following the murder, a rift developed between the Irish and French justice systems. Ireland insisted that there was no legally admissible evidence against Bailey. France, on the other hand, invoked its laws, which allowed a suspect to be convicted in absentia if there was sufficient circumstantial evidence; and that is exactly what happened years later.

Bailey had been arrested twice by the Irish police, once in 1997 and again in 1998. In both instances, he was released after a short time. The public prosecutor's office refused to press charges due to a lack of evidence. It was a slap in the face for Sophie's family. The Irish authorities justified their actions, while the media increasingly picked up on the case. Bailey, who continued to work as a journalist, was interviewed by many broadcasters. He responded in a bizarre, self-deprecating manner, as if he were enjoying the attention.

Not everyone in the community was on his side. Many neighbors kept their distance from him. Some testified under oath that Bailey had been violent toward his partner in the past. Others reported that he had repeatedly implied, while drunk, that he had "killed someone." Bailey himself later claimed that these statements were sarcasm, a kind of dark humor, but in the context of the murder, they seemed more like disturbing confessions.

Over the years, the case became a political issue. Irish media regularly reported on new developments, French newspapers called for justice, and relations between the countries were tense. In 2001, France submitted an official extradition request for Ian Bailey, which Ireland refused. There was no formal charge, and Irish law protected its citizens from extradition without valid grounds.

Despite all the disappointments, Sophie's relatives did not give up. They organized memorial events, set up a foundation, and kept alive the memory of the woman whose life had been so brutally ended. Sophie's son, Pierre-Louis, who had been a teenager at the time, became his mother's committed advocate, both figuratively and legally.

In the meantime, Bailey remained a free man, but the shadows were growing longer. Documentaries, podcasts, and true crime shows took up the case. Again and again, Bailey was the focus of attention. Some saw him as a victim of a media witch hunt, others as a manipulative and intelligent perpetrator who exploited the weaknesses of the system.

Then, almost two decades after the crime, something suddenly happened that brought the case back into the public eye, this time internationally.

On May 27, 2019, the most significant legal step in the case to date was taken in Paris: Ian Bailey was charged in absentia before a French criminal court. Based on the available files and witness statements, the French judiciary had decided to proceed with the trial even without the physical presence of the defendant; a legally permissible option in France when extradition cannot be enforced.

The trial lasted several days, with more than 20 witnesses heard, including former friends, neighbors, police officers, investigators, and members of Sophie's family. The evidence remained circumstantial, but the testimony painted a consistent picture of a man with violent tendencies, contradictory statements, and a disturbing proximity to the crime scene.

On May 31, 2019, the Paris Assize Court announced its verdict: Ian Bailey was found guilty of murdering Sophie Toscan du Plantier on December 23, 1996, in Toormore, West Cork. The sentence: 25 years in prison.

But the verdict remained symbolic. Bailey remained in Ireland, and the Irish government again refused to extradite him, this time on the grounds that he had already been arrested twice in Ireland for the same crime but had not been charged. Extradition would violate Irish law and the principle of double jeopardy.

Bailey himself reacted to the verdict with his usual mixture of defensiveness and provocation. In interviews, he called the trial a "farce" and a "legal nightmare." He continued to deny any involvement in the murder and increasingly presented himself as the victim of a political and media campaign.

In France, however, the verdict was seen as an important step. For Sophie's family, it was the first step toward justice, even if the convicted man was not behind bars. Her son, Pierre-Louis, said in an interview: "The verdict cannot bring my mother back. But it shows that she has not been forgotten."

The French government again called on Ireland to reconsider its position, but Dublin stuck to its line. In addition, Bailey successfully appealed against his extradition several times. The European arrest warrant issued against Bailey had no practical effect in this case. The case highlighted the limits of cross-border prosecution and the powerlessness of the judiciary when legal systems clash.

For Bailey, the legal pressure was real, but hardly noticeable in his everyday life. He continued to live in West Cork, published poems, appeared occasionally on television, and seemed to enjoy the attention. For many observers, this was a grotesque situation: a convicted murderer who had never seen the inside of a cell, and yet had traumatized an entire country.

Even after the French conviction, Ian Bailey remained at large in Ireland. The years passed, but the case continued to haunt people in France and in Ireland. There were repeated reports of new investigations, inconsistencies in the investigation, and old witnesses making new statements. Documentaries began to pile up. Netflix and Sky released lavishly produced series about the murder, and Bailey himself gave interviews in which he protested his innocence.

But his public image had changed. Where there had once been a certain fascination, he was now increasingly seen as a symbol of a failed justice system; someone who had slipped through the loopholes while a family had still not received any real justice.

Sophie's son appeared repeatedly on television shows, gave lectures, and publicly advocated for judicial reform. He was firmly convinced that Bailey was his mother's murderer and that it should never have come to this. The bitter reality was that no one had the power to bring the man who took his mother's life to justice.

Over the years, Ian Bailey's life became more turbulent. He lost his partner, Jules Thomas, who had supported him for years despite everything. In 2020, they separated for good. Bailey was reported several times for minor offenses, including drug possession and harassment. His mental state was considered increasingly unstable.

There was also repeated discussion of possible mistakes made at the crime scene. Important evidence had not been secured. Potential witnesses had not been interviewed in a timely manner. And Bailey? The man who was one of the first on the scene never really disappeared from the public eye, even though his guilt was never legally proven in Ireland.

Over time, a grim picture emerged: a brutal murder in a peaceful place, a prime suspect who was never brought to justice, a family waiting for justice, and a rule of law that functioned so differently in two countries that in the end no one knew what was truth and what was tragedy.

On January 8, 2023, it became known that Ian Bailey was struggling with serious health problems. The local press reported heart failure and several hospital stays. He himself admitted in an interview that he only had a few years left to live. His voice was fragile, his attitude wavering between defiance and resignation. "I am not a murderer," he said repeatedly. And yet he was the man who had been convicted in France for the murder of Sophie Toscan du Plantier, and who remained free in Ireland until his death.

On January 21, 2024, Ian Bailey died of a heart attack at the age of 66. It happened on a park bench in the center of Bantry, not far from the coast that had been his home for so long. His death brought the case back into the headlines, and with it the questions that had never been answered.

For Sophie's family, Ian Bailey's death was no consolation. There was no admission of guilt, no final truth, no apology. Pierre-Louis said in a television interview just a few days after Bailey's death: "Now that he is gone, we hope that the memory of my mother will not fade. That she is more than an unsolved criminal case."

In fact, in the years following her death, Sophie Toscan du Plantier had taken on a special role in the collective memory. She became a symbolic figure: for female victims of violence and for inadequate international judicial cooperation.

In Ireland, too, there was now a discussion about whether a belated legal review was still possible. Whether, despite Bailey's death, certain investigative errors should be made public. But many had long since lost faith in ultimate justice.

Today, a simple wooden cross stands at the spot where Sophie's body was found. Tourists hiking through the hills of West Cork often stop, read her name, and some lay flowers. The wind blows across the fields, just as it did on that night shortly before Christmas.

Watch the video

A profiler's opinion on this case

CASE 24

24. DECEMBER

On December 24, 2007, while all of America was preparing for Christmas, something unimaginable happened in the small community of Carnation, Washington. On a remote farm, nestled between snow-covered fields and festively decorated houses, an entire family was wiped out – six people, including two small children. The perpetrators: the family's own daughter, Michelle Anderson, and her partner, McEnroe.

That morning, everything seemed calm. The parents, Judy and Wayne Anderson, an elderly, reclusive couple, were preparing their house for the traditional Christmas dinner. Their son Scott had announced that he would be coming with his wife Erica and their two children, Olivia and Nathan. Only their eldest daughter, Mary, was ill and unable to come. Anderson and McEnroe also lived on the property, not in the main house, but in a trailer that stood a little apart.

It was no secret that the relationship between Anderson and the rest of the family was tense. For years, she had been considered difficult, quarrelsome, and dissatisfied. Nevertheless, her parents continued to support her financially and emotionally. But on this Christmas Eve, something had changed. Out of frustration, anger, or jealousy—perhaps all of the above—Anderson decided she'd had enough.

Around 4 p.m., she and McEnroe left their trailer, armed with two pistols. Judy was outside wrapping presents when McEnroe engaged her in conversation. At that moment, Anderson snuck up behind her with her gun drawn. Wayne, who was sitting in the house, noticed the scene through the window and rushed outside, but it was too late. A fatal shot to the head from McEnroe (Anderson's gun jammed) ended his life, with Judy being shot seconds later.

The bodies were hastily dragged into a nearby barn. Anderson and McEnroe knew they had to act quickly. Within an hour, Scott would arrive with his family – and they too would not survive the evening.

At around 5 p.m., Scott's car drove up the driveway to the Andersons' farm. With him were his wife Erica, five-year-old Olivia, and three-year-old Nathan. They were looking forward to celebrating with their grandparents – nothing suggested that the house they knew so well had already become a crime scene. Anderson greeted the arrivals with a fake smile, explaining that her parents had gone out to do some last-minute shopping. No one was suspicious. The family entered the house.

Scott and his family took a seat in the living room. The children ran around curiously. In the next second, several shots rang out. Anderson had suddenly pulled out her gun and shot her brother in the head. He was killed instantly. Erica screamed, grabbed the children, and ran away—but Anderson and McEnroe were close behind. In her panic, Erica managed to barricade herself and the children in a room. There she grabbed the phone and dialed 911.

But the connection had barely been established when McEnroe broke down the door. The young mother begged for her children's lives, but McEnroe shot her in the head before destroying the phone; the children were now alone. Five-year-old Olivia clung to her mother's motionless body. Nathan, just three years old, didn't understand what was happening. He picked up the phone batteries and handed them to McEnroe – a final innocent act that cost him his life. McEnroe shot the little boy in the face.

On that Christmas Eve, three generations of the family were wiped out. No warning, no reason. Just pure hatred and blind obedience to Anderson—a woman who called herself "the white crow"—a victim, she claimed, who had been unjustly cast out. But it was not rebellion; it was a cold-blooded massacre.

At 5:13 p.m., Erica had dialed 911, but her call was not completed. Nevertheless, the connection was enough to alert the police. A patrol car was sent to the farm. When the officers arrived shortly thereafter, they encountered Michelle Anderson, who calmly approached them and claimed that everything was fine. She even demonstratively locked the gate in front of their eyes. Despite the obvious tension at the scene, the police were unable to force entry. The farm remained locked for the time being, and the officers left.

On December 26, the crime was finally discovered. Judy Anderson did not show up for work. Her colleague Linda was worried and drove to the remote property. When she arrived, she saw that both families' cars were still there. There were no lights on, the house appeared empty – and yet the front door was unlocked. A pungent smell hit her as soon as she entered. When she reached the basement, she discovered several motionless bodies in the darkness – at first, she thought it was gas poisoning.

As she approached one of the bodies, she saw the head wound. Then she realized the full extent of the tragedy: four bodies, carelessly piled on top of each other. Linda immediately called 911 from a landline phone. Within minutes, the police were on the scene—and this time they stayed. In the basement, they found Scott, his wife Erica, and their two children. In the barn were the bodies of the parents, Judy and Wayne. All had been executed by shots to the head.

Around 11 a.m. that same day, Michelle Anderson and her boyfriend Joseph McEnroe returned to the property. Apparently, they believed they had sufficiently covered up the traces of the crime. But what awaited them was a full police operation, crime scene tape around the house, and officers who immediately confronted them.

During questioning, Anderson initially claimed that they had not been in town on December 24. They had wanted to travel to Las Vegas to get married, but had gotten lost. However, the couple could not produce any travel documents or a marriage certificate, nor were they wearing rings.

McEnroe became increasingly nervous. The investigators sensed that something was wrong – and when they put pressure on him, he broke down. After just a few minutes, he confessed. Crying, trembling, and with a broken voice, he explained that he had killed the family. He called himself a "monster" and said he could no longer live with it.

The confession came like a dam bursting. He described the crime in frightening detail. Anderson confessed shortly afterwards – but without tears, without visible remorse.

She soon followed with her own version – cool and calculating, but equally clear. They talked not only about the murders, but also about the alleged motives.

Anderson said she hated her brother. Scott owed her $40,000 over the years, a sum that was demonstrably fabricated. Her parents had not supported her, had even pressured her to pay rent for her trailer park space. And then she said something that her boyfriend repeated several times, which deeply shocked the investigators: she had killed her little niece and nephew because she wanted to spare them "growing up in a cruel world."

In truth, it was envy. Wounded pride. The desire to take revenge for years of insults, whether imagined or real. Her statements were contradictory, her emotions difficult to grasp, but one thing was obvious: Anderson had planned this crime, not in a moment of anger, but over weeks. And she had convinced her partner to follow her to the bitter end.

Both were cooperative. They led investigators to the place where they had disposed of the two murder weapons: a river near the farm. Divers recovered the pistols, and a ballistics report confirmed that they had been used to shoot the family.

Then the reconstruction of the crime began. On December 24, around 4 p.m., the couple had armed themselves with pistols and waited for the moment when their parents were alone. Then they killed them, followed by the rest of the family.

After the brutal crime, Anderson and McEnroe tried to cover their tracks. They cleaned the house as best they could, hid the bodies of Judy and Wayne in the barn, and carelessly stacked the bodies of Scott, Erica, and the children on top of each other in the basement. It was a macabre attempt to maintain control over the chaos they themselves had created.

But time was working against them. When Anderson and McEnroe returned to the farm on the morning of December 26—supposedly to start the day "as normal"—they were met by the police.

The trial of Michelle Anderson and Joseph McEnroe became one of the most sensational criminal cases in the history of Washington State.

The prosecution detailed how Anderson had built up a grudge against her family over many years. She felt like an outsider, unloved, and disadvantaged. McEnroe, who was described as quiet, submissive, and mentally unstable, followed her unconditionally. Together, they planned the extermination of their family—on Christmas, one of the most symbolic and peaceful days of the year.

During the trial, Anderson appeared uninvolved for long stretches. She occasionally cast mocking glances at the audience, seemingly unaware of the gravity of her actions or unwilling to face it. McEnroe, on the other hand, cried often. He repeatedly apologized to the relatives, asked for forgiveness, and said he lived every day with what he had done.

Despite his remorse, the verdict was clear. McEnroe was found guilty on all six counts of first-degree murder. In 2015, he was sentenced to life in prison without the possibility of early release. In the trial against Michelle Anderson, the jury also found her guilty on all counts—she too was sentenced to life in prison.

The family that was wiped out by this murder consisted of loving, kind people. Wayne and Judy Anderson were considered generous, helpful parents. Scott was a responsible husband and father, and Erica was a warm-hearted and dedicated mother. The young children, Olivia and Nathan, were cheerful, curious, and full of joie de vivre—their futures brutally extinguished before they could really begin.

Today, a memorial stone commemorates the victims of the Carnation massacre. It stands not far from the farm where the murders took place. Friends, neighbors, and relatives gather there every year at Christmas to lay flowers and fill the silence of the snow-covered landscape with a quiet promise: that they will never be forgotten.

Watch the video

A profiler's opinion on this case

Printed in Dunstable, United Kingdom

72894162R00127